THE
LAST
NIGHT OF
BALLYHOO

THE LAST NIGHT OF BALLYHOO

Alfred Uhry

THEATRE COMMUNICATIONS GROUP

The Last Night of Ballyhoo is published by Theatre Communications Group, Inc., 355 Lexington Ave., New York, NY 10017.

Cover design by Carol Devine Carson.

Cover photograph courtesy of the Alliance Theatre Company from the William Breman Jewish Heritage Museum.

Uhry, Alfred.
The last night of Ballyhoo / Alfred Uhry
ISBN 1-55936-140-9
1. Antisemitism—Southern States—Drama. I. Title.
PS3571.H7L37 1997
812'.54—dc21   97-40179
                                                                      CIP

Book design and composition by Lisa Govan.

First Printing, November 1997

For my mother and father

The Last Night of Ballyhoo opened on July 20, 1996, at the Olympic Arts Festival in Atlanta, Georgia, where it was presented by the Alliance Theatre Company (Kenny Leon, Artistic Director). The production was directed by Ron Lagomarsino. The set design was by John Lee Beatty; costumes were by Susan E. Mickey; lighting was by Kenneth Posner; music was composed by Robert Waldman; sound was by Brian Kettler; the stage manager was Bradley McCormick. The cast was as follows:

LALA LEVY	Mary Bacon
REBA FREITAG	Valerie J. Curtin
BOO LEVY	Dana Ivey
ADOLPH FREITAG	Terry Beaver
JOE FARKAS	Stephen Mailer
SUNNY FREITAG	Jessalyn Gilsig
PEACHY WEIL	Stephen Largay

The Last Night of Ballyhoo opened on Broadway on February 27, 1997. The production was directed by Ron Lagomarsino. The set design was by John Lee Beatty; costumes were by Jane Greenwood; lighting was by Kenneth Posner; music was composed by Robert Waldman; sound was by Tony Meola; the stage manager was Franklin F. Keysar. The cast was as follows:

LALA LEVY	Jessica Hecht
REBA FREITAG	Celia Weston
BOO LEVY	Dana Ivey
ADOLPH FREITAG	Terry Beaver
JOE FARKAS	Paul Rudd
SUNNY FREITAG	Arija Bareikis
PEACHY WEIL	Stephen Largay

Originally produced on Broadway by Jane Harmon, Nina Keneally and Liz Oliver.

CHARACTERS

Adolph Freitag, a businessman, late 40s
Boo Levy, Adolph's sister, a few years older
Reba Freitag, Adolph's sister-in-law, middle 40s
Lala Levy, Boo's daughter, 20s
Sunny Freitag, Reba's daughter, 20
Joe Farkas, Adolph's business assistant, 20s
Peachy Weil, a visitor from Lake Charles, 20s

TIME

December 1939

PLACE

Atlanta, Georgia

The action takes place in Adolph Freitag's house, at
the Standard Club, and aboard the Crescent Limited.

ONE

SCENE ONE

Lights up on Adolph Freitag's house on Habersham Road. It is mid-December 1939. We see a portion of the living room, a hall with stairs leading to the bedroom floor, and a portion of the dining room beyond the hall. The house is vaguely Spanish—stucco with a tile roof, Moorish archways, wrought-iron railings, etc. The furnishings are many and heavy.

Lala Levy is decorating a Christmas tree in a corner of the living room, surrounded by cardboard boxes of ornaments. There are a few strings of Christmas tree lights strung across the furniture. Lala is an unsure, awkward young woman. There is a slightly desperate air about her.

Reba Freitag, Lala's aunt, is on the sofa, knitting a sweater. Reba is in her middle forties, a pretty, vague woman, not quite in synch with everybody else.

LALA *(Singing as she decorates)*:
> Nooo-elll
> Nooo-elll
> Nooo-elll

Nooo-elll
Born is the King of Israel!

REBA: Lala?

LALA: Yes?

REBA: I forgot what a sweet singing voice you have.

LALA: Thank you, Auntie.

REBA: Like a little bird.

(Beulah "Boo" Levy enters from the hall, an apron over her sensible housedress. She is a serious woman, about fifty or so.)

BOO: Oh God!

LALA *(Singing)*:
They look-ed up and saw a star
Shining in the east beyond them—

BOO: Lala!

LALA: How do you like the tree so far, Mama?

BOO: Where did that star come from?

LALA: I bought it at Rich's.

BOO: Take it down!

LALA: Why?

BOO: Take it down this minute!

LALA: I like it.

BOO: Jewish Christmas trees don't have stars.

LALA: Why not?

BOO: You know perfectly well why not.

REBA: A star is a symbol of the birth of the Messiah.

LALA: Oh pooey.

BOO: If you have a star on the tree, you might as well go back on down to Rich's and buy a manger scene and stick it in the front yard.

LALA: I'd like that.

BOO: Fine. Then everybody that drives down Habersham Road will think we're a bunch of Jewish fools pretending we're Christian.

REBA *(Knitting away)*: Yes, they will.

LALA: What do you mean? We have a big Christmas tree right here in the front window!

BOO: A Christmas tree is another thing altogether. It's a festive decoration like a Halloween pumpkin or a Valentine heart. Everybody with any sense in their head knows that Christmas is just another American holiday if you leave out all that silly nonsense about Jesus being born. Now take down that star.

LALA: I wish you two could see yourselves!

REBA: Is my hair funny?

LALA: Atlanta is the center of the world tonight and you two are goin' at me over a Christmas tree ornament. We ought to be celebrating.

BOO: Celebrating what, I'd like to know.

LALA: My God, Mama! Clark Gable is less than five miles from this house right this very second.

BOO: And precisely what does that have to do with us?

REBA *(Checking her knitting)*: Drat!

LALA: Tonight is the most important event in the history of Atlanta!

BOO: For Margaret Mitchell, maybe. But not for me and certainly not for you.

REBA: I did something wrong. I'm never going to get this sweater finished in time for Sunny to take back to college!

LALA: Why certainly not for me?

BOO: You have other things to think about.

LALA: What.

BOO: Ballyhoo.

LALA: Ballyhoo is ages away.

BOO: Less than two weeks. And nobody's asked you.

LALA: I don't care!

BOO: I do.

LALA: Then get somebody to ask you! And leave me alone!

BOO: Phone Sylvan Weil in Lake Charles. That's all I ask.

LALA: Mama!

BOO: Well why not?

LALA: Girls don't ask boys to Ballyhoo.

BOO: I didn't say ask him. I said telephone him and after you've chatted for a while, you can inquire about his plans for the holidays—casually.

LALA: I don't care what his plans are for the holidays.

BOO: Of course you do. You and he are good friends.

LALA: We are not good friends. We are acquaintances.

BOO: Acquaintances? What about that house party at Myrtle Beach? And he's certainly all you talked about when you came home from Edith Asher's wedding in Birmingham last month.

LALA: He's all you talked about. "A Louisiana Weil! A Louisiana Weil! Finest family in the South. Weil Weil Weil Weil Weil."

BOO: There is nothing wrong with good bloodlines.

LALA: Maybe—if you're breedin' cocker spaniels.

BOO: I'm sure he's a lovely boy.

LALA: He's not very romantic.

BOO: Well, Lala, let's face it. Clark Gable is probably not going to ask you to Ballyhoo.

LALA: But somebody else just might.

BOO: Who?

LALA: Ferdy Nachman.

REBA: Oh, I wouldn't go around with him if I were you.

LALA: Why not?

REBA: His father picked his nose during his own wedding ceremony.

BOO: What does that have to do with anything?

REBA: I was a bridesmaid. I saw it. Dr. Solomon was just about to say the blessing and all of a sudden out of the corner of my eye, I saw Max Nachman take his index finger and—

BOO: Reba, for God's sake!

REBA: Well— *(She goes back to her knitting)*

BOO: Ferdy Nachman is four years younger than you.

LALA: So what?

BOO: You'd be a laughingstock.

LALA: Sez you!

BOO: Call Lake Charles!

LALA: I've got to get ready to go. *(She starts out of the room)*

BOO: Where are you going?

LALA: To town.

BOO: Town! For what?

LALA: The premiere.

BOO: You don't have a ticket to the premiere.

LALA: I don't care! I'll get to see everything.

BOO: You mean you're planning to go down there and stand out in the street?

LALA: Yes!

BOO: Are you crazy?

LALA: I want to feel the excitement in the crowd! To taste it! To smell it!

REBA: Why would you want to smell a lot of people you don't know?

BOO: She doesn't mean that literally, Reba.

REBA: Oh.

BOO: It's the most ridiculous thing I ever heard of—running off downtown by yourself in the dark.

LALA: You don't understand. I have to.

BOO: Have to?

LALA: Yes.

BOO: Why?

LALA: Well, I might as well go ahead and tell you the news.

BOO: What news?

LALA: I'm writing a novel!

BOO: Oh my Lord!

LALA: It takes place in Atlanta during the Reconstruction period and the title is "Though Your Sins Be Scarlet"!

REBA: Well I swan! Good for you!

LALA: But now promise me y'all won't say a word about it to anybody until the publication date is set.

BOO: Publication date! How much of this novel have you written?

LALA: I know exactly how it's going to end, and I thought of the first sentence this afternoon. "From where she sat atop the weathered buckboard wagon, Ropa Ragsdale could see the charred and twisted remains of her beloved plantation."

REBA: Ropa Ragsdale!

LALA: My heroine—short for Europa. I found it in a book of poems. Anyway, that's why I have to go be at the premiere.

BOO: Exactly what is why?

LALA: Well, Mama! Obviously my novel will more than likely be made into a movie. So I need to go and see what all a premiere is like.

REBA: The child has a point, Boo.

BOO: She does not have a point. And I'll thank you to stay out of this. Lala, for the life of me I don't know why you waste your time with all this utter foolishness when you could easily do something so much more constructive.

LALA: Like what?

BOO: Phone that Weil boy in Lake Charles.

LALA: Mama!

BOO: I know what I'm talking about.

LALA: My novel is not foolishness!

BOO: Your novel does not exist and the Weil boy does.

REBA: Your Mama has a point.

BOO: You didn't listen to me up at the University of Michigan and look what happened. You got so humiliated—

LALA: That wasn't my fault.

REBA: It was that awful sorority.

BOO: The fault does not lie with Sigma Delta Tau. You didn't prepare for rush week.

LALA: Mama!

BOO: I told you to prepare some peppy and interesting topics to discuss, and of course you paid me no mind and look what happened. You were rejected.

LALA: I was accepted in A.E.Phi.

REBA: That's true.

BOO: Hah! A.E.Phi! Nobody but the other kind belongs to A.E.Phi and the whole world knows it.

LALA: I don't want to talk about it anymore.

BOO: You'd better. You keep making the same mistakes over and over! Your place in society sits there waiting for you and you do nothing about it.

LALA: Guess what, Mama? We're Jews. We have no place in society.

BOO: We most certainly do! Maybe not right up there at the tip-top with the best set of Christians, but we come mighty close. After all, your great-grandma's Cousin Clemmie was—

(Here Lala joins in, and they say the next sentence together.)

BOO AND LALA: The first white child born in Atlanta!

LALA: God knows I've had that information drilled into my skull enough times.

BOO: Then why hasn't it sunk in? Why won't you use your connections and your birthright to make something of yourself instead of mooning over nonsense like tree trimming and movie premieres?

LALA: Only you could manage to ruin Christmas and *Gone With the Wind* in one fell swoop. *(She rushes out of the room and up the stairs)*

REBA *(After a discreet silence)*: Poor thing. I think she must be constipated.

BOO: Well, something is certainly the matter with her. I

mean, how hard can it be to pick up a telephone and place a call to Lake Charles, Louisiana?

REBA: Her head is full of that novel she's writing.

BOO: Reba, Lala is no more writing a novel than I am entering the Miss Georgia Beauty Contest.

REBA: Well, she said she was!

BOO: Yes. And last month she said she was making scripts for *Our Gal Sunday* to go on the radio. And before that she said she was becoming an illustrator for *The Saturday Evening Post*! I think she dreams up all that trash just to torture me! Doesn't she know that life is passing her by? She's the only girl in her crowd not married.

REBA: The Dahlman girl isn't married.

BOO: Well, of course she's not married. How could she be married? She's in Milledgeville in the insane asylum!

REBA: People get married in insane asylums all the time.

BOO: That's jails, Reba. People get married in jails.

REBA: Oh.

BOO: And Babette Dahlman was never in Lala's crowd to begin with.

REBA: She most certainly was.

BOO: What? I ought to know who was and who wasn't in my own daughter's crowd.

REBA: Then how come you invited her to that Easter egg hunt you had for Lala at the club that time?

BOO: That was twenty years ago! They were two years old!

REBA: I don't want to talk about it anymore.

BOO: I blame Lala's whole situation on the red measles.

REBA: Unh-hunh.

BOO: She was the cutest little baby there ever was. She had so many birthday-party invitations in nursery school that I ran out of ideas for presents to give. And then, the first week of kindergarten, she came down with the red measles. The very first week! And of course by the time she was well enough to go back to school, all the popular children had formed their attachments and no matter how she tried, or I tried for her, she was never able to catch up.

REBA: And she's such a sweet little thing!

BOO: Then why is she so unpopular?

REBA: Well, she gets herself so worked up when she's out in society. I think she scares people off.

BOO: And now this Ballyhoo business.

REBA: Heavens, Sunny doesn't have a date to Ballyhoo either, and I never give it a second thought.

BOO: Sunny has college to occupy her mind. I tell you, Reba, sometimes I can almost hear God sittin' up there in the sky giggling his head off at the joke he played on me.

REBA: I never thought of God playin' jokes.

BOO: Well, what else would you call it? You have a daughter bloomin' like a rose at Wellesley and I have a daughter who snuck home in disgrace from the University of Michigan in the middle of her first term. I was never so embarrassed in my life.

REBA: She said she was homesick.

BOO: And luckily everybody in Atlanta believed it.

REBA: Luckily? It's common knowledge that homesickness is a serious problem in your family.

BOO: It is not!

REBA: What? You were so homesick on your wedding trip that DeWald had to bring you back home from Point Clear five days early.

BOO: That's the silliest thing I ever heard in all my life. DeWald was called home for a business meeting.

REBA: I know that's what you said to everybody, but your mother told me the truth.

BOO: What truth?

REBA: Didn't I ever tell you this? The day before your brother and I married, your mother said to me, "Now, Rebecca, I don't want you making a fool of yourself on your wedding trip and mortifying everybody in the family like Beulah did." And of course I didn't. Simon and I stayed our full two weeks at Tybee Island.

BOO: Yes. And Simon told Mama what happened on your wedding night. And Mama repeated it to me.

REBA: I don't know what you're talking about.

BOO: Simon told Mama he came to get in the bed with you on your wedding night and you were sitting there with a thermometer stuck in your mouth.

REBA: I felt flushed. I didn't want him to catch anything.

BOO: Talk about making a fool of yourself on your wedding trip!

REBA: What are you doing?

BOO: What do you mean what am I doing?

REBA: Well, look at you. You're just throwing clumps of tinsel at that poor tree. It's supposed to go on strand by strand.

BOO: Thank you. I didn't realize I had the honor of decorating with a tinsel expert.

(Adolph Freitag enters the hall. He is a man in his late forties, soft body, hard mind—a pillar of the business community. He wears a double-breasted suit and a white-on-white monogrammed shirt. He carries a briefcase and the evening paper.)

ADOLPH: Evenin'.

BOO: Evenin', Adolph.

ADOLPH: Tree looks fine.

REBA: Thank you, kind sir.

ADOLPH: Star's a new addition.

BOO: Ain't it grand? Compliments of Lala. Don't worry. We had words about it and it's coming down.

ADOLPH: I like it.

BOO: Oh, Adolph. You do not.

ADOLPH: Sorry. I keep forgetting. You know the inner workings of my mind better than I do. Do I smell noodle soup?

BOO: You smell Brunswick stew.

ADOLPH: Good. We've got company.

REBA: Company?

ADOLPH: Asked a fulla home from the office.

BOO: You know Louisa's been out sick all week! You could have phoned me.

ADOLPH: We'll manage.

BOO: We will, will we? What time is he coming?

(The front doorbell rings. Adolph admits Joe Farkas, a vigorous young man in his twenties. He has a New York accent.)

ADOLPH: Joe Farkas. My sister-in-law, Mrs. Freitag.

JOE *(Shaking Reba's hand)*: How are ya.

ADOLPH: And my sister, Mrs. Levy.

JOE *(Shaking Boo's hand)*: How are ya.

BOO: How do you do.

JOE: No complaints!

BOO: Is this your first visit to Atlanta, Mr. Farkas?

ADOLPH: He ain't visiting, Boo. He's working for me.

BOO: Since when?

ADOLPH: Few weeks ago.

BOO: I see. *(To Joe)* My brother's real good at separating the family business from the family. He keeps everything concerning the Dixie Bedding Corporation a deep, dark secret. He thinks we're too stupid to understand anything.

JOE: Maybe he's just protecting you.

ADOLPH: Maybe I'm just protecting the Dixie Bedding Corporation.

BOO: You might ask my brother sometimes who worked like an Egyptian slave when the company first started.

ADOLPH: I bet he can guess.

JOE: You were at Dixie Bedding?

BOO: Until I married.

JOE: Oh yeah? Doin' what?

BOO: Probably just about what you're doing now. *(To Adolph)* Am I allowed to know what Mr. Farkas does, or is it too complicated for my tiny brain to grasp?

JOE: Joe, if you don't mind.

ADOLPH: He's gonna do some traveling for me, look in at some of the stores, take care of a few things here.

BOO: I see. My brother obviously has plans for you, young man.

JOE: Joe.

REBA: You surely picked an exciting time to be in Atlanta, Mr. Farkas. *(She catches herself)* Joe.

JOE: Yeah. They were putting up police barricades all over the place downtown tonight. That must be some movie they got there!

REBA: We have tickets for this Sunday afternoon!

JOE: No foolin'!

BOO: What part of New York City are you from, Joe?

JOE: You got a good ear, Mrs. Levy! Eastern Parkway.

BOO: Mmm-hmmm.

REBA: Now I wonder if you know my cousin Nellie Nadler from Charleston. She's married to a man named Charles Himmelfarb and they live at eleven-o-six Madison Avenue. I always remember that because Nellie's birthday is November the sixth. Eleven-six and eleven-six.

BOO: I believe Eastern Parkway is in Brooklyn, Reba.

JOE: Right again.

REBA: Oh.

BOO: He couldn't possibly know your cousin Nellie.

JOE: I don't know her, Mrs. Freitag, but I bet she's a nice lady.

REBA: She is. And she makes every stitch of her clothes by hand, except her girdles and her brassieres.

BOO *(To Reba)*: Reba, I need you in the kitchen.

REBA: Our cook has been home sick all week.

JOE: I hope I'm not causing you too much trouble.

REBA: Oh no!

BOO *(With a look at Adolph)*: None whatsoever.

(Boo and Reba go through the dining room and offstage.)

ADOLPH: Piece of the paper, Joe?

JOE: Thanks.

(Adolph sits in his easy chair and picks up the front section of the paper. He hands the second section to Joe. Adolph opens his section and disappears behind it. The huge banner headline deals with the Gone With the Wind *opening. Joe looks at his section of the paper, ill at ease.)*

JOE *(After a bit)*: I'm afraid I got a confession to make to ya, Mr. A.

ADOLPH *(Behind his newspaper)*: Oh yeah? What's that?

JOE: I'm a little bit out of my element here.

ADOLPH: Element?

JOE: Um, this *Gone With the Wind* stuff.

(Adolph lowers his paper, peers at Joe.)

ADOLPH: You never read *Gone With the Wind*?

JOE: Um, no. Unh-unh.

ADOLPH: A man after my own heart.

JOE: You didn't either?

ADOLPH: Well, I flipped through a few pages a coupla times, but I never could make myself get the hang of it.

JOE: No kidding.

ADOLPH: Don't tell anybody.

JOE: You bet.

ADOLPH: Settled at the Y all right?

JOE: Yessir. Thanks for the tip. Even found a coupla guys to play handball with.

ADOLPH: Good.

JOE: 'Course my mom wasn't too thrilled about a nice Jewish boy living at the Young Men's Christian Association.

ADOLPH: Yeah?

JOE: I told her "Relax, Ma. Whaddaya think, they put conversion powder in the tap water?"

(Lala comes down the steps, dressed to go out. Joe jumps to his feet.)

ADOLPH: Joe Farkas, new fulla works at the office. Lala, my niece.

JOE: Good to see ya.

LALA: Hey.

ADOLPH: You off somewhere?

LALA: The world premiere.

ADOLPH: By yourself?

LALA: Honestly, Uncle Adolph! 'Course not! Eugene Selig and Harold Lillienthal both asked me. I couldn't make up my mind which one to pick, so we're all three going together.

ADOLPH: I see. Well, it's too bad Joe didn't know in time. He's a big fan of *Gone With the Wind!*

LALA: Really?

JOE: Your uncle is teasing. Truth is, I haven't gotten around to reading it yet.

LALA: I bet you're the only person in this town who can say that.

ADOLPH: Absolutely.

JOE: Sounds like you got an exciting evening ahead of you.

LALA: Yes.

JOE: The premiere and everything.

LALA: I tell you what. Let's you and I eat here with the folks and then we can go downtown together and see all the celebrities come out when the movie's over.

JOE: I wonder what your two boyfriends would say to that?

LALA: Gene and Harold? Fiddle dee dee! They can just have a date with each other, for all I care.

JOE: Gee, you shouldn't do that on my account.

(Reba, carrying dishes of food, comes into the dining room from the kitchen. She puts the dishes on the table.)

REBA *(Calling)*: Supper's served!

(Adolph puts his newspaper down and walks into the dining room, where he begins to pick from the serving dishes with his fingers. Boo enters with more food. Lala and Joe walk toward the table.)

LALA: I never met a Farkas before.

JOE: Yeah. I seem to be a rare bird down here.

LALA: Is that a New York City name?

JOE: More or less.

LALA: Oh good! You must know all the smart supper clubs in Manhattan.

JOE: Well, truth is, I—

LALA: What's your favorite?

JOE: Never been to one in my life.

LALA: I need to know. I'll more than likely be going to New York very soon.

JOE: No kidding. What for?

(Boo sees Adolph picking at the serving dishes and slaps his hand.)

BOO: Stop that!

LALA: To meet with publishers about the novel I'm writing.

BOO: Oh my God!

ADOLPH: Let's eat.

REBA *(Raising her water glass)*: Welcome to Atlanta, Joe!

(Lights out.)

SCENE TWO

When the lights come up again, it is an hour later. Dinner is over.

   Reba is making trips on- and offstage from the dining room, clearing the table. Lala and Joe are in the living room. Adolph is back in his easy chair with the newspaper, dozing.

LALA: Do you want to hear it?

JOE: Uh, sure.

LALA: "From where she sat atop the weathered buckboard wagon, Ropa Ragsdale could see the charred and twisted remains of her beloved plantation."

JOE: Good. Real good.

LALA: At first I had "old family home," but I think "beloved plantation" has more charm, don't you think?

JOE: Right.

LALA: Except I need a name for the plantation. Something elegant and pure and real Protestant. *(She thinks a minute)* I think I have it!

JOE: What?

LALA *(With reverence)*: Habersham Hall! Isn't that beautiful? Habersham Hall!

JOE: Unh-hunh. After your street here.

LALA: I wasn't thinking of it that way, but yes! Of course! This is just about the best address in Atlanta. Did you know that?

JOE: Not really.

LALA: You have only to look at the mailboxes up and down this street and you'll see half the membership of the Junior League!

JOE: Huh!

LALA: I'll have you know that we are the only Jews on Habersham Road except for one house way on the other side of Paces Ferry, where it gets tacky.

JOE: Um, you think your uncle is okay?

LALA: Of course. He's just having what we call his presnooze snooze. He does this all the time.

JOE: I'm not surprised if they always feed him like that.

REBA *(From the dining room)*: We know good food in this house. Nobody would deny that.

JOE: I sure wouldn't.

REBA: Neither would my Sunny.

JOE: Sonny?

REBA: My daughter.

JOE: Daughter?

REBA: That's right.

JOE: Sonny's a boy's name in my neighborhood.

REBA: Not that kind of Sonny. *(She points straight up)* That kind of Sunny. Because she was born in the middle of a terrible storm.

JOE: I don't get it.

REBA: Well, we certainly couldn't name her Cloudy, could we?

JOE: Um, no. I guess not.

(Boo enters the living room, taking off her apron.)

BOO: Louisa just better come back to work tomorrow. That's all I have to say.

JOE: I would've been glad to help, Mrs. Levy. I know my way around the kitchen pretty well.

BOO: You?

JOE: Yes ma'am.

BOO: Who ever head of such a thing?

JOE: Oh, my mom had me and my brothers drying dishes soon as we could stand on a stool and reach the sink.

LALA: That's adorable.

BOO: If you want half your china broken.

JOE: We all cook too. She taught us to make a few staples from the old country.

LALA: Old country?

JOE: Russia, Poland, Hungary. My family came from everywhere.

BOO: Adolph has never crossed the threshold of a kitchen in his life. Except to pick out of the icebox in the middle of the night.

ADOLPH: Ain't I the limit?

(Reba finishes in the dining room and comes into the living room.)

REBA: There. That's all of it.

JOE: Why isn't your daughter here, Mrs. Freitag?

REBA: She's away at school.

LALA: Wellesley.

JOE: Really?

LALA: She got the brains. I got the moxie.

JOE: Oh, a little bird tells me you went to college, too.

LALA *(Suddenly panicked)*: What?

JOE: College.

LALA: College? Who told you about that?

JOE: About what?

BOO: Lala attended the University of Michigan for a short time, but she missed all the social goings-on here so much that home she came.

LALA: Yes. Home I came.

BOO: And we were thrilled to have her.

REBA: Tell me, Joe, will be going up to your home for Christmas?

JOE: No ma'am. My boss there keeps me hoppin' too much for that. But it's okay. My family doesn't celebrate Christmas.

BOO: I see.

JOE: I'll be home for Pesach, though.

LALA: Pesach?

JOE: Passover.

BOO: You remember, Lala. That time we went to the seder supper with one of Daddy's business acquaintances. I believe their name was Lipzin. They lived over on Boulevard or somewhere. You were in the sixth grade. It was very interesting.

LALA: I was in the fifth grade, and I spilled a glass of red wine all over the tablecloth.

JOE: Right. One of us does that almost every year. Part of the ritual.

LALA: You have to sit through one of those boring things every single year? One night of all that ish-kabibble was enough to last me the rest of my life.

BOO: Now, Lala. Be tolerant.

JOE: I sit through two every year. First night at Aunt Sadie's. Second night at home.

LALA: Poor baby!

JOE: Are you kidding? I wouldn't miss either one of 'em for anything in the world.

REBA: Now, they have those in the spring, don't they?

JOE: Yes ma'am. That's right. March or April.

LALA: Good. Then you'll be here for Ballyhoo.

BOO: Lala!

JOE: What's Ballyhoo?

LALA: What's Ballyhoo? Why, Joe! What a question! But of course you are a Yankee!

REBA: The young people come from all over the South.

LALA: Savannah and Chattanooga and Charleston.

REBA: Even Richmond and New Orleans.

JOE: I got it. Like a convention.

LALA: Oh no.

REBA: Not at all like a convention. No name tags, or talks or business meetings of any kind.

LALA: Hayrides and weenie roasts and parties, and, the last night, a dance.

JOE: Don't say!

REBA: It all started in Macon.

BOO: It started in Gulfport.

REBA: I happen to know it started in Macon. Matille Lowenstein was there.

BOO: Of course she was there. She's always there. She lives in Macon.

REBA: A bunch of young people were having a picnic on Matille's sister-in-law's side porch after the second daughter's wedding to that Kriegsauber boy from Chattanooga the summer after the war ended. I believe it was the Fourth of July weekend, and Matille told me they were enjoying each other so much that they decided they would all get together again in Atlanta at Christmastime.

BOO: Matille Lowenstein is a known liar.

REBA: Why, Boo! She was in my confirmation class! She's a lovely girl.

BOO: Matille Lowenstein isn't worth the gunpowder it would take to blow her up. It started in Gulfport after

Mr. Nathan Solomon's ninety-fifth birthday party. It was all his grandchildren and the Rosenheim boys that thought it up.

REBA: It started in Macon.

BOO: Adolph? Adolph? *(She shakes him awake)*

ADOLPH: What?

BOO: Tell this young man where Ballyhoo started.

(Adolph looks at Boo for a minute.)

ADOLPH: What the hell would he care about a stupid thing like that?

LALA: Oh, I think he might care a little. Am I right, Joe?

JOE: Well yeah. It's very interesting.

LALA: 'Specially if you're planning on going this year.

JOE: Going? Oh. Say, it must be gettin' late.

LALA: Silly! It's not even nine o'clock! The movie's still on. We have oodles of time to drive downtown and see the stars come out! And then we can meet the crowd at the Ansley Roof.

JOE: You know, that sounds like a lotta fun, Lala. But I got a train to catch at six-thirty in the morning, so I better call it a night.

LALA: But—

BOO: No, sugar pie. You heard Mr. Farkas. He has a train to catch in the morning and all the important Dixie Bedding Company business to attend to. He really must be going. *(To Joe)* So good to have met you.

JOE: Yeah. Great meal, Mrs. Levy. You too, Mrs. Freitag. 'Night, Mr. A.

ADOLPH: Have a safe trip, Joe.

JOE: So long, Lala. 'Night, all.

(Joe exits. A momentary silence.)

REBA: Well now, never you mind.

LALA *(Trying to stay calm)*: Mind? Mind what? I believe I'll go on up to my room and see what's on the radio. *(She goes out into the hall)* Stop looking at me. *(She runs up the stairs)*

BOO: Adolph, that kike you hired has no manners.

(Lights out.)

SCENE THREE

In the dark, we hear the voice of a railroad conductor.

CONDUCTOR: Baltimore. The stop is Baltimore. Baltimore coming up!

(Lights up on a small sleeping compartment of the Crescent Limited, five days later. Sunny Freitag, twenty years old, is alone, reading a book. She is attractive, reserved.
There is a knock on her compartment door.)

SUNNY: Yes?

(Joe enters, wearing a hat and a topcoat.)

JOE: You Miss Freitag? Sunny Freitag?
SUNNY: Yes?
JOE: Joe Farkas. Pleased to meet you.

(He holds his hand out pleasantly. She shakes it warily.)

SUNNY: I—I don't understand.

JOE: Uncle Adolph asked me to look in on you.

SUNNY: What?

JOE: See if you need anything.

SUNNY: Oh. *(A beat)* Thank you.

JOE: What?

SUNNY: What?

JOE: What do you need?

SUNNY: Oh. Nothing.

JOE: Because he gave me a little extra cash to give you if—

SUNNY: No.

JOE: Sure?

SUNNY: Yes.

JOE: Okay.

SUNNY: Thank you. *(She goes back to her book, expecting him to leave)*

JOE: What're you reading?

SUNNY: Um, *The Profits of Religion.* Upton Sinclair.

JOE: Upton Sinclair, hunh? The glorious unwashed masses and the beauty of the working class. You really enjoy reading this stuff?

SUNNY: Yes.

JOE: Eugene V. Debs too?

SUNNY: Yes.

JOE: Oh boy!

SUNNY: What?

JOE: I sure didn't peg you for a Communist.

SUNNY: Reading Sinclair and Debs doesn't make a person a Communist.

JOE: You don't know my Uncle Velvel.

SUNNY: Uncle what?

JOE: Velvel.

SUNNY: Velvel?

JOE: Jewish for William.

SUNNY: Oh. Well, I'm not a Communist.

JOE: That's a relief!

SUNNY: I'm a sociology major.

JOE: Wellesley, I know.

SUNNY: Who told you?

JOE: Your family. I work for Mr. A.

SUNNY: Mr. A.?

JOE: Uncle Adolph.

SUNNY: In Baltimore?

JOE: Atlanta.

SUNNY: You don't sound like Atlanta.

JOE: Sorry.

SUNNY: No! I didn't mean—I just—never mind.

JOE: You do.

SUNNY: I do what?

JOE: Sound like Atlanta. It's nice.

SUNNY *(Embarrassed)*: Oh.

JOE: So I happened to be in town here on a little business and Mr. A. said would I mind giving you a look-see in case you needed something. What's the matter?

SUNNY: Nothing.

JOE: Come on.

SUNNY: It boggles the mind.

JOE: What?

SUNNY: I'm a junior at Wellesley with an A-minus average and Uncle Adolph still treats me like a baby.

JOE: Why do you say that?

SUNNY: He doesn't even think I can take a train home by myself.

JOE: Oh, I think he just loves you a lot. And I really did just happen to be in Baltimore. So how come the minus?

SUNNY: What?

JOE: You mentioned your average was A minus.

SUNNY: I had trouble with zoology last year. What was yours?

JOE: Zero. Didn't go. Well, I did, kind of. I went to art school.

SUNNY: Don't they have grades in art school?

JOE: I guess. I was only there for five weeks.

SUNNY: Why?

JOE: My father died. I had to go to work.

SUNNY: Oh no! I'm so sorry!

JOE: Yeah. Well, it was a long time ago.

SUNNY: I hope you kept up with your artwork.

JOE: When I get the chance. I guess you've got a lot lined up over Christmas vacation.

SUNNY: A lot of work.

JOE: So you won't be going to this Ballyhoo thing?

SUNNY: Did Uncle Adolph tell you about that?

JOE: No. Your cousin, Lala.

SUNNY: Really?

JOE: Yeah, and she was dropping plenty of hints.

SUNNY: Hints?

JOE: I think she wants me to take her.

SUNNY: Oh. And?

JOE: I pretty well sidestepped the issue.

SUNNY: You were smart.

JOE: How's that?

SUNNY: Ballyhoo is asinine.

JOE: Yeah? Why?

SUNNY: Oh, you know, a lot of dressed-up Jews dancing around, wishing they could kiss their elbows and turn into Episcopalians.

JOE: Sounds pretty terrible.

SUNNY: It is.

JOE: Wanna go with me?

CONDUCTOR: *(Offstage)* All aboard! All aboard.

(Joe moves toward the door.)

JOE: Word is I'm a good dancer.

SUNNY: I'm not.

JOE: Baloney. I gotta get to work. Think it over.

(He smiles, leaves. She looks after him.
Lights fade.)

SCENE FOUR

The Freitag house. It's 8 A.M. the following morning. A pile of wrapped presents is under the Christmas tree, which is now minus its star. The remains of breakfast are on the dining room table, where Adolph sits with his coffee, going over some paperwork. Reba, in a housecoat, is cleaning up.

Boo comes in from outdoors carrying the morning paper, which she hands to Adolph. She appears to be agitated.

BOO: I just saw Louisa.

REBA: Well praise be! I was afraid she would never recover.

BOO: Recover? Hah! She never was sick.

REBA: What are you talking about?

BOO: I saw her when I went down the driveway to pick up the *Constitution*. She was going up the Arkwrights' driveway across the street.

REBA: I don't understand. Why was she doing that?

BOO: That's what I asked her. I said, "Aren't you walking up the wrong driveway, Louisa?"

REBA: And what did she say?

BOO: She said no she was walking up the right driveway because she works for the Arkwrights now.

REBA: How can she work for them when she works for us?

BOO: What is the matter with you, Reba? She doesn't work for us. She quit! That's what I'm telling you.

REBA: Oh. *(She thinks about this for a second)* Why?

BOO: I asked her. I said, "Why"? And she looked me in the face cold as ice and she said, "You know exactly why." And then she said to tell you hey and that she knows she has your red umbrella and she'll get it back to you.

REBA: How sweet.

BOO: Sweet? You'll never see that umbrella again as long as you're walking on this earth! I can promise you that! Louisa is a liar! Standing there in the street right up next to my face and telling me I know why she snuck off and abandoned us. I have no idea in the world what she was talking about!

REBA: Well—

BOO: Well what?

REBA: You did accuse her of stealing pocket change off of Adolph's bureau. I heard you.

BOO: I did no such thing. I merely pointed out to her that the money was missing and inquired politely if she knew what had happened to it.

REBA: All right, then.

BOO: Louisa is probably over there telling the Arkwrights all kinds of stories about us right this very minute. And Mary Grace Arkwright already looks at me like I have horns and a tail! I don't know how I'm ever going to be able to go down the driveway again.

REBA: I think you have to give Louisa more credit. I'm sure she will have something nice to say about your peach ice cream. She's crazy about your peach ice cream.

BOO: Well all I know is that it's four days before Christmas and we'll never find anybody worth having now.

REBA: I suppose.

BOO: We may never find anybody at all, what with Louisa running her big mouth to every single solitary maid, cook and chauffeur riding back and forth to work on the Peachtree Trolley with her.

REBA: Oh, I feel sure we'll be able to find somebody perfectly fine after the first of the year.

BOO: Yes. And you and I are stuck with all the picking up, all the cleaning, all the cooking and all the everything else in the meantime.

ADOLPH *(Calling from the dining room)*: Why not?

BOO: Did you say something, Adolph?

ADOLPH: I said, why not? What else do you have to do so much? You ready to go, Reba?

REBA: I'm all dressed but my dress. *(She goes up the stairs and exits)*

BOO: What's the matter with you?

ADOLPH: This Hitler business in Poland. Ain't gonna turn out good.

BOO: Oh stop worryin' about Poland so much and give a thought to your own flesh and blood for a change.

ADOLPH: What are you talkin' about?

BOO: That was a fine something to say to me!

ADOLPH: What?

BOO: That I don't have anything better to do than take care of this house.

ADOLPH: Just speakin' the truth.

BOO: And another thing, I don't see why you have to go running off to meet Sunny at the train. Reba is perfectly capable of finding Brookwood Station by herself.

ADOLPH: I don't have to. I want to.

BOO: You never meet Lala.

ADOLPH: I would if she went somewhere.

BOO: She went to that wedding in Birmingham last month. You make it sound like all she does is lie up there on her bed and listen to the radio.

ADOLPH: You said that. I didn't.

BOO: Lala does plenty. She took that literature course at Agnes Scott last year. She volunteers at Eggleston Hospital when she can. She has that regular Thursday afternoon bridge game.

ADOLPH: Fine.

BOO: Sunny isn't a direct pipeline to the Lord Almighty, you know.

ADOLPH: Who said she was?

BOO: That's how you treat her.

ADOLPH: For God's sake, Beulah! Maybe you forgot how Simon looked after us all when Papa died.

BOO: He had to. He was the oldest.

ADOLPH: Maybe he had to support Mama, but he didn't have to put me all the way through Tech and Lord knows he didn't have to buy you that trousseau you raised such hell over and all that damn sterling silver. That's when he was just getting Dixie Bedding started and I know for a fact that he didn't have two nickels to rub together. He must've borrowed and squeezed and cut all kind of corners. I know he worried himself sick over his obligations to all of us, and I know that's what landed him in Oakland Cemetery a good twenty-five years ahead of schedule and I'll be goddamned if I have to justify myself to you if I feel like meeting his daughter at the train when she comes home from college.

BOO: You get yourself so worked up. You'll be laying out there right beside Simon if you don't look out.

ADOLPH *(Calling upstairs)*: Reba! Hurry it up! We don't want to be late!

REBA *(Offstage)*: Right down.

BOO: Adolph! Calm down!

ADOLPH: I want to be there on time. Do you mind?

BOO: I mind how you do Lala. Her Daddy is every bit as dead and gone as Simon is.

ADOLPH: Yeah. Men don't stand much of a chance around here, do they?

BOO: And when I think of how you did him! Here you are fawning over that awful boy from Brooklyn—that Joe person—like he was the crown prince of Denmark and the only brother-in-law you ever had you treated like dirt.

ADOLPH: Beulah! That is not so!

BOO: Yes! You never gave DeWald a Chinaman's chance where Dixie Bedding was concerned. I always got better grades in arithmetic than—

ADOLPH: My God! Don't start bringin' all that—

BOO: Than either one of you. And what good did it do me? I was completely shut out of the business. Completely shut out!

ADOLPH: Did I ask you to marry and stay home! Did I ask you to have a baby? Did Simon? No. You did all that on your own without instructions from your brothers. And as for DeWald—we tried him in the front office. We tried him in sales. We tried him in the factory. You know that.

BOO: Maybe DeWald wasn't as smart as all of us, but he was a good man. And it was a shame how you two did him.

ADOLPH: Some shame! We damn well supported him most of his life.

BOO: Even now you can't say a decent word where he's concerned. It hurts my feelings.

(Reba comes down the stairs, dressed to go out.)

REBA: Do these shoes look funny?

BOO: No.

ADOLPH: Let's go, Reba.

REBA: Bye. *(She exits)*

ADOLPH: Boo?

BOO: What?

ADOLPH: DeWald had beautiful table manners.

BOO: That's more than anybody could ever say about you.

(He exits. After a moment, the telephone rings.)

BOO: Hello? What? This is Beulah Levy. Who is this? *(She listens. When she speaks again, it is with a much friendlier tone)* Sylvan Weil? Of course I know who you are, Sylvan! Your Aunt Ethel and I spent part of a summer together down at Point Clear! Oh, ages ago! Yes, we were just girls. Tell me, Sylvan, does she still have that limp? Well, bless her heart! Why, yes, Lala most certainly is at home. *(She calls in her most musical voice)* Lala! Oh, Lala! Telephone for you.

(Lala enters.)

LALA: What?

BOO *(Sotto voce)*: It's the Weil boy.

LALA: Peachy? *(She takes the phone)* Well, hey stranger. I thought you fell in a bayou or something. Unh-hunh. Peachy! What? You call that good news? I guess so. Peachy! Okay. Bye. *(She hangs up the phone)*

BOO: Well? What did he say?

LALA: He said to tell you he enjoyed meeting you over the phone.

BOO: What else?

LALA: He's coming to Atlanta.

BOO: I see. When?

LALA: The day before Christmas.

BOO: I knew it! Lala, did Sylvan Weil ask you to go to Bally-hoo with him?

LALA: Peachy, Mama! Everybody calls him Peachy.

BOO: He did, didn't he? He asked you!

LALA: He didn't mention Ballyhoo. He just said he'd be in Atlanta with his parents for the Zachariases' golden wedding anniversary party.

BOO: Of course. I should have thought of that. Mr. Ike Zacharias is his great-uncle. His father's mother was a Zacharias from Hattiesburg. Tell me, does he have ugly red hair?

LALA: Yes.

BOO: I was afraid of that. They all do. Well, we don't have to worry about it. In the great scheme of things, it could be a lot worse. Are you sure he didn't mention Ballyhoo?

LALA: Maybe he doesn't know about it.

BOO: Lala, every Jewish boy in the South with half a brain in his noggin knows about Ballyhoo. You should have brought it up.

LALA: Mama! Do you want me to sound desperate?

BOO: A fact is a fact, daughter. And the fact is it would be a shot in the arm to your situation to be seen at Ballyhoo with a Weil from Louisiana.

LALA: I don't have a situation.

BOO: The subject is closed.

LALA: I can do better than Peachy Weil.

BOO: No you can't.

LALA: I may have other plans for Ballyhoo.

BOO: You do not. Ferdy Nachman is taking little Carol Strauss. Her mother told me at the meat counter yes-terday afternoon. *(She picks up the phone)*

LALA: What are you doing?

BOO: I'm going to phone that Weil boy's Aunt Ethel and find out what's what.

LALA: Mama, you haven't been in touch with that woman for thirty years!

BOO: He told me she lives in Baton Rouge now. I wonder if she's married? She couldn't be with that limp.

LALA: Mama!

BOO *(Into the phone)*: Operator, connect me with Miss Ethel Weil in Baton Rouge, Louisiana.

(Lights fade.)

SCENE FIVE

The Freitag house. Eleven o'clock that night.
Sunny and Adolph are playing gin at a card table. Reba
sits nearby, knitting away on her argyll socks. There is a
feeling of warmth in the room. Adolph and Sunny play a
couple of tricks silently.

ADOLPH: Knock on six.

(He lays down his cards. Sunny does the same.)

SUNNY: No! Three—nine—twenty—that's twenty-three
points for you.

(He writes it down.)

I liked it when you used to let me win.
ADOLPH: I never let you win.
SUNNY: Then how come I used to beat you all the time?
ADOLPH: Maybe Wellesley is making you stupid.

SUNNY: Uncle Adolph!

REBA: Do you think that's possible, Adolph?

SUNNY: He's teasing me, Mama.

REBA: Because higher education can lead to insanity.

SUNNY: What?

(Sunny and Adolph exchange amused looks. He deals another hand, which they play out during the following.)

REBA: Yes. You remember, Adolph. One of the Feigenbaum girls.

ADOLPH: The Feigenbaum sisters! Who could forget?

REBA: They lived on Georgia Avenue just across from the trolley barn. There were seven of them. One more hideous than the next.

ADOLPH: And your mother is being generous.

SUNNY: She was insane because she was ugly?

REBA: Oh no! Not at all! In fact she was the least hideous one.

ADOLPH: There's a compliment for you.

REBA: Viola was her name. Viola Feigenbaum. And she was the smartest, too. At least, she was the only one that went on to college. She attended Peabody Normal.

SUNNY: Peabody Normal?

ADOLPH: In Nashville.

REBA: She was studying to be a teacher. But then she went crazy in the train.

SUNNY: Crazy in the train? What does that mean?

REBA: Well, her Papa put her on the N.C. & St. L. to Nashville so she could start her second year at Peabody Normal and she was as sane as you or I right this minute. Then one hour after they left Terminal Station, she took off every stitch of her clothes and ran up and down the aisle of the day coach naked.

SUNNY: Maybe she was hot.

REBA: I don't like your tone, Sunny. They had to make an unscheduled stop in Rome to remove the poor thing from the train, rolled up in a tablecloth!

SUNNY: That's awful! What became of her?

REBA: She married and moved to Louisville. Her husband and his whole family never knew a thing in the world about it.

SUNNY: They didn't hear through the southern Jewish grapevine? How is that possible?

REBA: Well, they were the other kind.

SUNNY: Other kind? Other kind of what?

REBA: You know perfectly well what I mean.

SUNNY: Explain it to me.

ADOLPH: Stop teasing your mother.

SUNNY: I'm not teasing. I really want to know.

REBA: East of the Elbe.

SUNNY: What?

REBA: That's how Grandma used to explain it.

SUNNY: What's the Elbe?

REBA: Well, I believe it's a river somewhere.

ADOLPH: Separates Germany from Czechoslovakia.

REBA: Yes. And west of it is us and east of it is the other kind.

SUNNY: But why are they the other kind?

REBA: Well—they just are.

SUNNY: How can you tell?

REBA: The way they look.

SUNNY: That's preposterous. Are you saying you could pick a hundred Jews off the street at random and tell who's what kind just by looking at them?

ADOLPH: Sure. The German Jews would be the ugly ones. I mean the men. And, of course, the Feigenbaum sisters.

SUNNY: It's a lot of mumbo jumbo and you both know it. And don't tell me they talk louder. Nobody talks louder than Aunt Boo.

ADOLPH: That's for sure.

SUNNY: And don't tell me they act funny, either, because—

REBA: Now don't you say one word about your cousin Lala. She does the best she can!

SUNNY: I rest my case. Gin.

(Adolph counts his points.)

ADOLPH: Twenty-four. I let you win.

SUNNY: You just now said you never let me win!

ADOLPH: So I did.

SUNNY: I really beat you then.

ADOLPH: Maybe. But I don't want you to feel good about it.

SUNNY: I missed you, Uncle Adolph.

ADOLPH: Yeah. How's school?

SUNNY: Fine, if you don't count botany.

REBA: You took botany last year.

SUNNY: That was zoology.

ADOLPH: What's the matter with botany?

SUNNY: Field trips! They're freezing!

REBA *(Knitting away)*: Well, I'm knitting as fast as I can!

SUNNY: I see that. Thank you, Mama. I stayed up so late studying for the last quiz that I got all mixed up.

ADOLPH: You did?

SUNNY: Yes. I said that leather grew on trees and rubber came from animals!

REBA: I think I'll go upstairs. *(To Sunny)* 'Night, Sugar. I'm just so glad you're home! 'Night, Adolph.

ADOLPH: 'Night.

(She gets up, starts out of the room, then turns.)

REBA: Isn't it silly! Askin' about rubber animals on a botany quiz!

(Reba exits up the stairs.

Sunny deals out another hand, and she and Adolph play it during the following. She sees Adolph looking at her.)

SUNNY: What?

ADOLPH: I went in your Daddy's office one morning to ask him a question about an ad we were gonna run. I'd say it was about twenty years ago. Anyway, I noticed he slid something he was looking at under a pile of manila folders real quick, like he didn't want me to see. And we talked about the ad a little bit, and all the time I kept looking at that pile of folders, wondering what the hell he was up to. I ever tell you this?

(She shakes her head no.)

So a couple of hours later, he went to the bank. And of course I hightailed it on into his office and I closed the door and I walked over to his desk and I moved the folders and guess what I saw.

SUNNY: What?

ADOLPH: A catalog from Smith, a catalog from Vassar and a catalog from Wellesley. He was researching colleges for you when you were six months old. Wouldn't he be tickled tonight?

(Lala and Boo come into the hall. Boo hangs up her coat. Lala keeps hers on.)

BOO: Hey.

SUNNY: Well, how was the movie?

BOO: Exactly the same as it was the other time.

LALA: Mama, how can you say that?

BOO: Oh, I'm sorry! Did Scarlett and Rhett do something different this time? I must've missed it.

LALA: That's not the point! Nobody can take in a masterpiece in one viewing. I came away with so much more tonight! I could watch it a thousand times.

ADOLPH: Y'know, I believe we're gonna make money out of you yet, Lala.

BOO: What are you talking about?

ADOLPH: The girl is a natural-born usherette.

BOO: Why, Adolph! *(To Lala)* He's joking, sugar. *(To Adolph)* Any calls?

ADOLPH: Calls?

BOO: For Lala.

LALA: Would you relax, Mama? You know Peachy's coming to Atlanta.

BOO: Well, I need to know more than that. I need to know for a fact he's taking you to the dance. And that aunt of his doesn't answer her phone. Why have you still got your coat on? Are you cold?

LALA: No.

(Boo feels her head.)

BOO: Are you catching something?

LALA: I already caught it.

BOO: I knew you weren't lookin' right. Where does it hurt?

LALA: Stop it, Mama. I'm not sick. I feel divine!

BOO: What in the world has got into you?

LALA: Remember in the intermission when you went to the rest room and I waited in the lobby?

BOO: Yes.

(Lala opens her coat and pulls out a 9" by 12" glossy photograph.)

LALA: Look!

BOO: Oh Goddy! How did you get that?

LALA: I was waiting for you to come out of the rest room. And I was looking at the pictures they had over in the corner. Scenes from the movie. And it looked like they were in frames. But they weren't. They were just slid in slots that looked like frames. So I slid one out!

BOO: I didn't see it.

LALA: I know. I slipped it under my sweater and then while you were watching Scarlett shoot the Yankee deserter on the stairs at Tara, I hid it in my coat.

ADOLPH: Usherette, hell! We can send her out in crowds to pick pockets.

BOO: This is not funny, Adolph. It's a crime.

SUNNY: Oh Aunt Boo! The Loews Grand isn't going to miss one silly photograph!

LALA: How dare you! It is not silly! It's Scarlett in her barbecue dress! It's magnificent!

SUNNY: Somebody's drivin' up the driveway.

BOO: Oh my God! It's the police.

LALA: I don't care! It was worth it!

ADOLPH: I feel pretty sure the Atlanta Police Department has better things to do than track down our little picture napper here.

BOO: Who would come driving up here in the middle of the night then?

(Doorbell sounds. Adolph opens the front door. Joe stands in the doorway holding a briefcase.)

JOE: I saw the lights on.

LALA: Well well! Look what the cat drug in!

JOE: Hiya. *(To Boo)* Ma'am. *(To Adolph)* I came right from the station. I brought you those sales figures from Washington.

ADOLPH: Yeah. Thanks. Could've waited till the office tomorra, y'know.

BOO: Certainly could've!

JOE: Well, I thought maybe you'd wanna give 'em a look-see tonight. And, like I said, I saw the lights.

ADOLPH: Yeah. Trip fine?

JOE: Yessir. I think I took care of everything. *(To Sunny)* Hi. How's our pal Upton Sinclair?

SUNNY: Oh, he's fine.

LALA: Upton who?

SUNNY: Nobody you know, Lala.

JOE: I see you got home in one piece.

SUNNY: Yes.

LALA: How come y'all know each other?

SUNNY: Uncle Adolph got Mr. Farkas to make sure I didn't fall off the train.

LALA: What?

ADOLPH: Looks like he did a good job. I don't see any bruises.

JOE: How was the rest of your train trip?

SUNNY: Fine, thank you. How was yours?

JOE: Not bad.

LALA: Seen *Gone With the Wind* yet, Joe?

JOE: No. Not yet.

LALA: It's a dream! Isn't it a dream, Mama?

BOO: Dreams don't last four hours.

SUNNY *(To Joe)*: You've done an awful lot of traveling in the past few days. You must be worn out, Mr. Farkas.

JOE: No, I'm fine. I'm used to it. And it's Joe.

SUNNY: Joe.

JOE: I like the way you say that.

BOO: Certainly late to be entertaining company.

ADOLPH: Why don't you go to bed then?

BOO: I didn't say I was sleepy. I said it was late to have company in the house.

JOE: I oughta be goin'.

BOO: Good night.

ADOLPH: Don't be silly. We can't send this boy off on an empty stomach! He's been traveling all day. We got any of that angel cake left from dinner?

BOO: Not after you attacked it.

ADOLPH: 'Course we do. Go on out in the kitchen and cut him a piece, and why don't you fix some coffee while you're at it?

JOE: Sounds good. I mean, if it's no trouble.

ADOLPH: 'Course it's no trouble.

BOO: Oh really?

SUNNY: I'll do it, Auntie.

LALA: You don't know how to fix coffee.

SUNNY: Yes I do. I make it in the dorm all the time.

LALA: I can imagine what that must taste like!

(Lala and Boo laugh.)

I'll do it, Uncle Adolph.

ADOLPH: Thank you.

(Lala exits. Boo walks out of the room, stops at the bottom of the stairs.)

BOO: Drinking coffee this late gives people gas. *(She goes up the stairs)*

ADOLPH: Come on in, Joe. You'll have to forgive my sister's bad temper. She was looking at Clark Gable for four hours and then she had to come home and look at me. Y'know, Joe, I used to be a travelin' man, just like you.

JOE: Don't say!

ADOLPH: When my brother was runnin' the company. Trains were a mess in those days. Windows wide open most of the year. Soot played hell with your collars and cuffs.

JOE: Yeah. I can imagine.

(A beat.)

ADOLPH: Well, I think I'm gonna go look over these sales figures. See you in the morning, Joe.

JOE: Yessir, Mr. A.

ADOLPH *(To Sunny)*: And if you do get gas, for God's sake don't let on to your Aunt Boo.

SUNNY: 'Night, Uncle Adolph.

(Adolph heads up the stairs. Sunny and Joe sit silently for a beat or so.)

SUNNY: Can I ask you something?

JOE: Shoot.

SUNNY: How did you get to Atlanta? And don't tell me you came on the train.

JOE: Actually I drove down. Okay, okay. I was selling mattresses at Macy's Herald Square and they offered me assistant bedding buyer at their store in D.C. and then the store across the street asked me to assistant manage and then that chain got taken over by Dixie Bedding and one day your Uncle Adolph came in to check us over and he hired me to work for him. That answer your question?

SUNNY: Yes.

JOE: Can I ask you something?

SUNNY: All right.

JOE: Are you people really Jewish?

SUNNY: 'Fraid so. A hundred percent all the way back—on both sides.

JOE: 'Fraid so?

SUNNY: Oh, you know what I mean.

JOE: Yeah. You mean you're afraid you're Jewish.

SUNNY: No. Of course not. That's just an expression.

JOE: Okay. What do you mean?

SUNNY: I don't think I mean anything. It was just something to say. Can we please talk about something else?

JOE: Sure. *(A beat)* Nice Christmas tree.

SUNNY: Thank you.

JOE: Old family tradition, is it?

SUNNY: I've had Christmas trees my whole life, if that's what you mean.

JOE: That's what I mean.

SUNNY: Is there something wrong with that?

JOE: Hey, I'm just trying to get the lay of the land down here. You know, smoke out the local customs.

SUNNY: Everybody I know has a Christmas tree. It doesn't mean we're not Jewish.

JOE: Right. It just means you don't wanna be.

SUNNY: Whether I want to be or not, I am, and there's not much I can do about it.

JOE: Sure there is. For starters you can anglicize your name.

SUNNY: Sunny Friday. Sounds like a weather report.

JOE: Or a striptease artist.

SUNNY: I could call myself Sunny O'Houlihan and everybody around here would still know what I am.

JOE: So what?

SUNNY: It hurts sometimes.

JOE: I know.

SUNNY: No. I don't think you do.

JOE: What do you mean?

SUNNY: I imagine you grew up in a Jewish neighborhood. You were like everybody else. I grew up on Habersham Road.

JOE: Only two Jewish mailboxes and the other one is down at the tacky end of the street where it doesn't count.

SUNNY: You've been talking to Lala.

JOE: Yep.

SUNNY: Well, see? That's all we wanted—to be like everybody else.

JOE: And you are.

SUNNY: Oh no. No we're not.

JOE: Whaddaya mean?

SUNNY: The summer between sixth and seventh grade my best friend was Vennie Alice Sizemore. And one day she took me swimming at the Venetian Club pool. Her parents were members. So we were with a whole bunch of kids from our class and the boys were splashing us and we were all shrieking—you know—and pretending we hated it, when this man in a shirt and tie came over and squatted down by the side of the pool and he said, "Which one is Sunny Freitag?" and I said I was, and he said I had to get out of the water. And Vennie Alice asked him why and he said Jews weren't allowed to swim in the Venetian pool. And all the kids got very quiet and none of them would look at me.

JOE: What did you do?

SUNNY: I got out of the pool and phoned Daddy at his office. When he came to get me all the color was drained out of his lips. I remember that.

JOE: And Vennie Alice?

SUNNY: Oh, her mother called up Mama and apologized. We stayed friends—sort of. Neither of us ever mentioned it again, but it was always there. So believe me, I know I can't hide being Jewish.

JOE: Yeah, so how come you try to camouflage it so much?

SUNNY: Oh, stop it! You think being Jewish means you have to run around in one of those little skullcaps and a long white beard?

JOE: Not in your case.

SUNNY: I'm serious!

JOE: Well, I guess I think being Jewish means being Jewish.

SUNNY: I wish you could've sat in on my comparative religions class last semester.

JOE: Why?

SUNNY: Professor Brainard made so much sense. She believes that all faiths are basically the same with different window dressings.

JOE: Really?

SUNNY: Yes. And I agree with her. I don't think what religion a person happens to be matters all that much in the modern-day world.

JOE: Oh, I think it matters to some pretty important people.

SUNNY: Like who?

JOE: Like Hitler.

SUNNY: No fair. Hitler's an aberration. Let's limit the discussion to human beings.

JOE: Tell you what. Let's drop it altogether.

SUNNY: Why?

JOE: Because I don't want to spend my first date with a pretty girl talking about Hitler.

SUNNY: This isn't a date.

JOE: Not yet.

SUNNY: What do you mean?

JOE: If I'm not mistaken, there's a White Castle right up there in Buckhead.

SUNNY: There is.

JOE: You hungry?

SUNNY: A little.

JOE: Great. Now it's a date!

SUNNY: Joe, I can't just go to Buckhead at this hour of the night.

JOE: Why not?

SUNNY: Mama wouldn't know where I am.

JOE: Leave her a note.

SUNNY: She's asleep.

JOE: Then what's the difference?

SUNNY: I don't do things like that.

JOE: Like what? Eat hamburgers?

SUNNY: I wouldn't feel right. I'm sorry.

JOE: Okay.

SUNNY: I know you're probably used to girls who—

JOE: Who what?

SUNNY: Take more chances.

(He thinks a minute.)

JOE: You think going out with me tomorrow night would be taking too big a gamble?

SUNNY: No, I imagine I can handle that.

JOE: White Castle in Buckhead?

SUNNY: Sure. And maybe a movie first.

JOE: One qualification.

SUNNY: What?

JOE: Not *Gone With the Wind*.

SUNNY: Agreed.

JOE: Good first date.

SUNNY: Yes.

JOE: And the second one is going to be even better.

SUNNY: Second one?

JOE: Ballyhoo. We made a deal, remember?

(Lala enters.)

LALA: The g.d. coffeepot boiled over, so it's gonna be a while.

JOE: It's okay. I really oughta go home and get some sleep.

LALA: You two made a deal?

JOE: We did.

SUNNY: Joe invited me to go to Ballyhoo.

LALA: I see.

JOE: However, before you commit to this a hundred percent, there's something you should know about me.

LALA: What?

JOE: I'm not as Jewish as you are.

SUNNY: What are you talking about?

JOE: I have royal Russian blood.

LALA: What?

JOE: There's a story in the family about my great-grandfather and the czarina's grand-niece, or was it my great-grandmother and the czar's third cousin?

SUNNY: Oh really?

JOE: Either way you should know you're going to the movies tomorrow night with part of a prince.

SUNNY: I'll work on my curtsey.

JOE: Yeah. You do that. So, how about it?

SUNNY: How about what?

JOE: Ballyhoo.

SUNNY: Okay.

JOE: Okay! Good night.

SUNNY: Good night.

JOE: Do me a favor.

SUNNY: What?

JOE: Say my name.

SUNNY: Joe.

JOE: I love it!

(He exits. Sunny locks the door after him. She starts turning out various lights during the following. Eventually the room is lit only by the Christmas tree.)

LALA: Well!

SUNNY: What?

LALA: He just barged in here in the middle of the night and made me go to all that trouble in the kitchen for nothing.

SUNNY: The coffee and cake were Uncle Adolph's idea.

LALA: Anybody brought up right would've known not to accept.

SUNNY: I offered to fix it.

LALA: That's not the point.

SUNNY: Oh. What is the point?

LALA: He's a very aggressive person.

SUNNY: Fine. Whatever you say.

LALA: And I certainly wouldn't be seen at Ballyhoo with him.

SUNNY: Luckily, that's a decision you won't have to make.

LALA: Meaning what?

SUNNY: Meaning nothing. I'm going to bed.

LALA: Not even twenty-four hours in the house and you're already lording it over me.

SUNNY: I'm not lording it over you. I'm just tired.

LALA: Poor Miss Wellesley. It must be so exhausting to have to deal with us piddling little inferiors.

SUNNY: I don't think you're inferior.

LALA: Yes you do. You always have.

SUNNY: This is pointless.

LALA: Remember your daddy's funeral?

SUNNY: What?

LALA: Uncle Simon's funeral—all those flowers and all those people—seven hundred I think the newspaper said. Mayor Hartsfield and that congressman and I don't know who all. Remember?

SUNNY: Of course. What about it?

LALA: Remember what I wore?

SUNNY: What you wore?

LALA: Yes.

SUNNY: What is wrong with you, Lala?

LALA: You don't remember. Why should you? Well, I remember what you wore to mine.

SUNNY: What?

LALA: My daddy's funeral. Three months later. Remember? That sad little biddy chapel with hardly anybody in it. And those pathetic gladiolas in back of the coffin. It was like a mockery of what your father had. And you wore an adorable navy-blue suit. Brand-new. So were the shoes. The soles weren't even scuffed.

SUNNY: Why would you remember a thing like that?

LALA: Because you wanted everybody to look at you!

SUNNY: I did not!

LALA: Nobody wears a whole new outfit unless they want to be looked at! That was supposed to be my tragedy! You already had yours and you had to have mine too!

SUNNY: That is a terrible thing to say!

LALA: But it's true, and you know it.

SUNNY: I know no such thing.

LALA: Oh come on, Sunny. You've always gotten all the attention. Even from God!

SUNNY: What?

LALA: He didn't give you one Jewish feature and look at me!

SUNNY: That's absurd.

LALA: Look at my hair! Look at my skin! Look at my eyes! Listen to my voice! I try and I try and no matter what I do it shows and there's just nothing I can do about it.

SUNNY: I wish you weren't so hard on yourself.

LALA: Well, you know what? You make it worse.

SUNNY: How?

LALA: You waltz into town for one day and finagle yourself an invitation to Ballyhoo.

SUNNY: My God, Lala! Why do you care so much about Ballyhoo?

LALA: You care just as much as I do.

SUNNY: I do not. I think Ballyhoo is a joke!

LALA: Then why are you going?

SUNNY: You want me to stay home?

LALA: Yes. You say you don't care about it. Stay home.

SUNNY: I will.

LALA: Good.

SUNNY: Fine. *(A beat)* No! I want to go!

LALA: I knew it! Hypocrite!

SUNNY: You are the biggest wet blanket in the world. No wonder nobody wants to take you to Ballyhoo.

LALA: Yes somebody does!

SUNNY: Oh really?

LALA: Yes. Really. And he happens to be a member of one of the finest families in the South!

SUNNY: Who is he?

LALA: You'll see, you'll see what happens when you come crawlin' to Ballyhoo with a pushy New York Yid tryin' to suck up to his boss and I sweep in with someone who belongs there. When I sweep in on the arm of a Louisiana Weil!

(Lights out.)

TWO

SCENE ONE

The Freitag house. The next morning.
   Boo is at her desk doing the accounting. Sunny is study-
ing. Reba is knitting, and Lala is pacing nervously.

BOO: Just call him.

LALA: I can't!

BOO: Why not?

LALA: Because.

BOO: We've got to make completely sure that he's taking you.

LALA: Phone his Aunt Ethel again.

REBA: She did. At quarter past six this morning.

BOO: How come you know so much about my business?

REBA: Because you woke me up, hollering so loud.

LALA: Quarter past six? That's quarter past five in Baton
   Rouge! How could you phone somebody up at quarter
   past five in the morning?

BOO: I wanted to make sure she wasn't there, which she
   wasn't. I can't imagine where in the world that silly
   woman could be keeping herself!

LALA: I can't either. I don't know why she hasn't been sitting right by the phone for the last thirty years waiting for you to call.

BOO: This is not the moment to run your sassy mouth. Time is of the essence. Will you call Sylvan or will I?

(After a moment, Lala picks up the phone and dials.)

LALA: Operator, I would like to place a long-distance call to Lake Charles, Louisiana. Person to person. To Peachy Weil. Not Miss. Mister. Mister Peachy Weil.

REBA: I didn't know you were allowed to use nicknames on long distance.

SUNNY: Oh, Mama! I do love you!

REBA: What did I say?

BOO: Y'all hush!

LALA: It's ringing! It's ringing!

(Lala listens. Boo hovers.)

No! *(She hangs up quickly)*

BOO: What?

LALA: I got the cook. She told the operator that Peachy's not there. She said he left this morning for Atlanta with his mother and daddy. We'll just have to wait until he gets here.

BOO: Oh no we won't. Move! *(She sits at the phone table, dials)* Operator. Get me the residence of Sylvan Weil Sr. in Lake Charles, Louisiana. Station to station. Weil. W-e-i-l.

LALA: I just told you! They're not there! What is the matter with you?

(Boo waves her away.)

BOO: Hello? Who is this? Well, hey Hattie. Merry Christmas to you. It's Mrs. Beulah Levy. No, I don't believe we do know each other. I'm an old friend of Mrs. Weil's in Atlanta. No, don't trouble yourself writing it down. I'll see her when she gets here. But do me a favor, would you, please? Run on up to Mr. Peachy's closet and see if he took his tuxedo with him. Would you do that for me? Thank you so much!

SUNNY: You're pretty brainy, Aunt Boo.

BOO: Yes. And, believe you me, if I were running the Dixie Bedding Company we'd all be rich by now.

REBA: We are rich, aren't we?

BOO *(In the phone)*: Yes. Yes I'm still here. I see. Sure do 'preciate it, Hattie. Unh-hunh. Good-bye. *(She hangs up. Triumphant)* The tuxedo isn't in his closet! And neither are his patent-leather dancing shoes!

LALA: I knew it! I always knew it!

REBA: Good for you, honey.

BOO: You're as good as at that dance, daughter! With the finest escort in the South!

LALA: Yes, Mama! Yes, I am! *(To Sunny)* I told you!

BOO: But what are you gonna wear?

LALA: I don't know, but it's gonna cost Uncle Adolph an arm and two legs. Come downtown with me.

BOO: I have the accounts to tend to, and a pot roast to do.

LALA: Let Aunt Reba! She won't mind!

BOO *(Sotto voce)*: Her pot roast tastes like shoe leather.

REBA: I'm not in Timbuktu, Beulah! I can hear every word you're saying.

BOO: Well, it's the truth.

REBA: Adolph loves my pot roast. He took thirds last time.

BOO: Adolph would take thirds of dog food if somebody stuck it on his plate.

LALA: Please come with me, Mama! You have such good taste in clothes.

BOO: Well. All right. *(To Reba)* Be sure you brown it carefully. On low heat. And for God's sake, stay away from the garlic.

(Boo and Lala start up the stairs.)

LALA *(As they go)*: Regenstein's had a dress in the paper this morning. "A holiday dream of glowing tulle and layered ruffles." What do you think?

BOO: It sounds like a lampshade.

(Boo and Lala exit.)

REBA: I will not stay away from the garlic. Garlic makes a pot roast. And your Aunt Boo knows it.

SUNNY: Then why would she say that?

REBA: Oh, she's just tryin' to make sure mine won't be as good as hers. I know her tricks.

(Sunny and Reba go into the living room, start folding newspapers, plumping sofa pillows, etc.)

REBA: It's a good thing we had babies at home in my day. That's all I have to say.

SUNNY: Why?

REBA: Because if you had been born in the hospital, I'd be 'fraid I brought home the wrong child.

SUNNY: Mama! What do you mean?

REBA: Well I just admire you so much, sugar! And I don't know where in the world you came from. You have so much sense.

SUNNY: Why, thank you!

REBA: And you certainly didn't inherit it from me.

SUNNY: Who says I didn't?

REBA: Well, all I know is if there'd been Ballyhoo in my day,

I would've probably carried on and acted as foolish as Lala. And here you are, perfectly content to stay home and study for your final exams and pay no mind to the whole silly rigamarole. My hat is truly off to you, sweetheart.

SUNNY: Mama?

REBA: Yes?

SUNNY: I am going to Ballyhoo.

REBA: You are! How nice! With who?

SUNNY: With Joe.

REBA: That good-looking boy who works for Adolph?

SUNNY: Yes.

REBA: Well, that's fine! And what are you gonna wear?

SUNNY: I was thinking maybe the blue velvet I wore in David and Virginia's wedding.

REBA: Yes. It's put away in the cedar closet.

SUNNY: I'll go get it out. *(She starts out of the room)*

REBA: You know, I wore blue the first time I went dancin' with your daddy.

SUNNY: Oh, Mama!

REBA: Well, go on up and air out that dress. You wouldn't want to go to Ballyhoo smellin' like a mothball.

(Sunny goes up the stairs; Reba continues with her cleaning.)

REBA *(To herself)*: She is a little bit like me! Thank the Lord!

(Lights out.)

SCENE TWO

That night. Adolph is asleep in the living room, the evening paper in his lap.

BOO *(Offstage)*: Adolph! Adolph!
ADOLPH *(Opening an eye)*: What?
BOO *(Offstage)*: Close your eyes!
ADOLPH: 'Kay.

> *(Adolph goes back to sleep. Boo comes down the stairs.)*

BOO *(Calling)*: Reba!
REBA *(Offstage)*: What?
BOO: You can finish in there later. We're ready.
REBA *(Offstage)*: All right!

> *(Reba comes in from the kitchen.*
> *In a moment, Lala descends the staircase in her formal; the dress is very* Gone With the Wind, *with a hoopskirt so wide she can barely get down the stairs.*

The price tag still hangs from the dress. Lala poses in the doorway to the living room.)

BOO: All right, Adolph. Open your eyes.

LALA: What do you think?

ADOLPH *(After taking in the scene)*: Well well well. Scarlett O'Goldberg.

LALA: Mama!

(Boo glares at Adolph.)

BOO: Adolph!

ADOLPH: Very nice, Lala. You'll be the belle of the ball, for sure.

LALA: Oh, Uncle Adolph! You're just saying that!

ADOLPH: No. I mean it. That's quite an outfit!

LALA: I'm so glad you like it. Because it cost a weensy bit more than we planned on.

(Adolph looks at the price tag.)

ADOLPH: It's all right. I can always get a night job.

BOO *(To Lala)*: He's just fooling, honey.

ADOLPH: Well, I'll say one thing. You won't have to worry about the boys gettin' fresh. They won't be able to come within six feet of you.

LALA: Oh, God! I never thought of that! What if I can't dance in it!

REBA: Don't be silly. It's a dancin' dress.

BOO: Well, of course it is!

(Boo and Reba start to hum "The Pink Lady Waltz" and Lala starts to waltz about the room. Lala waltzes up to Adolph.)

LALA: May I have this dance, sir?

(Adolph looks at Boo, sees there is no way out, and reluctantly starts waltzing with Lala. Sunny and Joe enter.)

REBA: See? I told you! The dress is fine! Sunny, look.
SUNNY: Lala, that's such a pretty dress.
JOE: Yep.
ADOLPH: Can we stop now?
LALA: Why, sir! You dance divinely!

(Lala continues pulling Adolph around the room.)

JOE *(To Sunny)*: Shall we?
SUNNY: I'd be delighted.

(Sunny and Joe start dancing, too, still in their hats and coats. Joe hums loudly and happens to be a wonderful dancer.)

JOE: What's this thing called?
SUNNY: The Purple Lady Waltz, I think.
REBA: The Pink Lady Waltz!
SUNNY: I was close.

(Joe accidentally steps on Lala's dress. She screams.)

LALA: It tore! He tore my beautiful dress.
BOO *(To Joe)*: You do nothing but cause trouble in this house, Mr. Farkas. *(To Adolph)* I hope you're happy! *(To Lala)* Come on. Come on, sugar baby.

(Boo helps Lala out of the room; they begin to go up the stairs.)

(Turning back to the others) You couldn't even let her have her joy for five minutes.

(They exit.)

REBA: It's just a little bitty rip. I'm sure it can be fixed. *(She hurries after them)*

JOE: Geez, I'm sorry, Mr. A.!

ADOLPH: Ah, forget about it.

JOE: I can pay for the dress.

ADOLPH: That's good because I can't. Look, I told you— forget about it.

SUNNY: Aunt Boo just overdramatizes sometimes.

ADOLPH: Sometimes? She's the Jewish Tallulah Bankhead.

SUNNY: You better hush before she comes down here and really lays into you.

REBA *(Offstage)*: Sunny, come up here and see what you think.

SUNNY: Okay, Mama. *(She goes upstairs)*

JOE: Your sister doesn't like me much, hunh?

ADOLPH: Nope. She don't like anybody very much, if that's any comfort.

JOE: But me especially.

ADOLPH: Oh yeah? What makes you say that?

JOE: I'm too Jewish.

ADOLPH: You are?

JOE: Come on, Mr. A. You know damn well that's the reason.

ADOLPH: I'm not my sister's keeper. Well, I guess I am my sister's keeper, but I'm not responsible for what she thinks.

JOE: You know, back up in my neighborhood who judges? Who cares? They're just Jews.

ADOLPH: Makes sense.

JOE: They like it. They're proud of it. And they're always trying to claim everybody.

ADOLPH: What do you mean?

JOE: You know, ballplayers, movie stars. Half the discussions around our dinner table were about who is and who's part. My Great-aunt Gussie swears that Franklin Roosevelt's real family name is Rosenfeld.

ADOLPH: Sounds like a good healthy attitude.

JOE: Listen, Mr. A., I gotta talk to you.

ADOLPH: Fine.

JOE: About this Ballyhoo business.

ADOLPH: Is there a problem?

JOE: Yeah. The tickets.

ADOLPH: I gave them to Sunny.

JOE: That's the problem.

ADOLPH: Why?

JOE: I want to pay for them.

ADOLPH: No.

JOE: Then I don't go.

ADOLPH: You don't understand. They were complimentary.

JOE: Yeah, sure.

ADOLPH: Really, they were.

JOE: Why's that?

ADOLPH: I'm a past president of the club. They send me free tickets to everything that goes on there.

JOE: The club?

ADOLPH: Standard Club.

JOE: Country club, right?

ADOLPH: Well, it would be if it was in the country. Right now it's a town club with delusions of grandeur.

JOE: Sounds pretty spiffy.

ADOLPH: I wouldn't say that.

JOE: Jews only?

ADOLPH: You bet.

JOE: No Christians allowed?

ADOLPH: Technically, but the truth is none of 'em would wanna come anyway. They've got clubs of their own, which they won't let us near.

JOE: So this is where all the Jews go.
ADOLPH: Oh no. We're restricted too.
JOE: What do you mean?

(Adolph looks uncomfortable.)

ADOLPH: Um, I mean membership is restricted to the well padded. As you can clearly see by the girth of the ex-president. Also well-padded in the monetary sense, of course.
JOE: I guess I'm a long way from joining, hunh?
ADOLPH: Who knows?
JOE: Still I pay my way to this dance or I don't go.
ADOLPH: I have no idea what the tickets are worth.

(Joe takes out his wallet, hands two bills to Adolph.)

JOE: This oughta cover it.
ADOLPH: And then some. I must be giving you too much salary.

(Sunny, coming down the steps, sees the money exchange.)

SUNNY: Uncle Adolph, are you bribing him to take me out?
ADOLPH: Other way around. He insists on paying for Ballyhoo. How's the great ball-gown tragedy?
SUNNY: All better. Mama saved the day.
JOE: Tell your cousin I'm really sorry.
SUNNY: I did. She forgives you.
JOE: I'm such a klutz!
SUNNY: A what?
JOE: You don't know what a klutz is?
SUNNY: Sorry.
ADOLPH: Means clumsy, don't it?

SUNNY: Is that Yiddish?

JOE: It's not Norwegian.

SUNNY: Uncle Adolph, I'm impressed! I didn't know you spoke Yiddish.

ADOLPH: About five words.

SUNNY: That's five more than me.

JOE: Well, I guess I caused enough trouble around here for one night. I better go. Gotta put in a decent day's work tomorrow.

SUNNY *(To Adolph)*: Are you making him work on Christmas Eve?

ADOLPH: You bet.

SUNNY: Scrooge!

JOE: G'night, Mr. A.

ADOLPH: Yeah.

(Joe touches Sunny's face lightly.)

JOE: 'Night, Sunshine.

SUNNY: Good night.

(Joe exits.)

ADOLPH: Sunshine?

SUNNY: Yes.

ADOLPH: People call you that?

SUNNY: No. He made it up. He's very imaginative.

ADOLPH: Must be.

SUNNY: And he's such a good dancer!

ADOLPH: I noticed.

SUNNY: And he has such beautiful hands.

ADOLPH: Now that I didn't notice.

SUNNY: So graceful! And so strong! And he's very bright, I mean, don't you think? For someone who didn't even go to college.

ADOLPH: You don't have to sell him to me, Sunshine. I was sold before you were.

SUNNY: Good.

ADOLPH: I probably shouldn't say this. In fact, I know I shouldn't say this, because you're very young and it's basically none of my business, and also it would send your Aunt Beulah to Piedmont Hospital, but I really think you should hold on to this boy. I don't think they come along any finer.

SUNNY: I don't think so either.

ADOLPH: I know Simon would approve.

SUNNY: I do, too. *(A beat)* Uncle Adolph?

ADOLPH: Yes?

SUNNY: Can I ask you something?

ADOLPH: Of course.

SUNNY: Were you ever in love?

ADOLPH: Oh yes.

SUNNY: What was her name?

ADOLPH: I never found that out.

SUNNY: You were in love with somebody and you never found out her name?

ADOLPH: Well, I didn't really know her. She used to ride the same Chatahoochee Avenue Streetcar as I did every morning. First summer I went to work with your daddy.

SUNNY: What did she look like?

ADOLPH: She had beautiful hands. They were little and soft—almost round. She had a pocketbook she held in her lap—with both of those pretty hands. And she had a whole lot of brown hair wound around on top of her head. She was always sitting there when I got on and after a week or two, she'd smile over at me after I sat down. Not every morning, but sometimes. Just the tiniest hint of a smile.

SUNNY: That meant she wanted you to talk to her.

ADOLPH: I don't think so. She smiled at everybody that same way.

SUNNY: I hope you at least smiled back.

ADOLPH: I did. I even smiled first once, but she got embarrassed and looked away, so after that I just waited for her.

SUNNY: And you never spoke to her?

ADOLPH: Sort of. One day when it was real hot, I ran my hand across my forehead and shook my head and she did the same thing back. And I thought we'd just naturally fall into a conversation after that, but then, a couple of days later, I got on the streetcar and she wasn't there. And she was never there again.

SUNNY: What happened to her?

ADOLPH: I have no idea. I asked the motorman, but he didn't even know who I was talking about. Imagine that! A beautiful girl like her—getting on and off of his car every single day and he never even noticed.

SUNNY: And there never was anybody else?

ADOLPH: Not really. I went with some girls, and I suppose I could've married one of 'em, but in the back of my mind I was waiting for somebody like the girl on the streetcar.

SUNNY: She was the love of your life.

ADOLPH: Yeah. And you know why?

SUNNY: Why?

ADOLPH: I never saw her for more than twenty minutes at a time and I had no dealings with her whatsoever.

SUNNY: Stop it. You'd make somebody a wonderful husband.

ADOLPH: Just what I need—another female to live in this house!

(Lights fade.)

SCENE THREE

The Freitag house. Eleven A.M. Christmas Day. The dining
room table is set for cake and coffee with the good silver
and china. A homemade coffee cake sits on a cake pedestal
in the center of the table. All that remains of the Christmas
presents are ribbons, paper and discarded boxes.

Boo is putting the living room in order. Reba is standing
in the open front door, speaking to someone outside. She
holds a red umbrella and a small wrapped gift.

REBA: Thank ya. Thank ya. Thank ya. And don't you be a
stranger over here now. Okay bye-bye. And tell all the
Arkwrights Merry Christmas. *(She closes the front*
door, unwraps the gift—a jar of preserves. She comes
into the living room) Look. Isn't this the sweetest thing!
Louisa put up watermelon pickles for us. And there's a
card. *(She reads)* "Happy Holidays to you and Mr.
Adolph and both the girls." I'm sure she means you,
too, Boo.

BOO: What do I care? I hate watermelon pickles!

REBA: And see? You were wrong about the umbrella. It's as good as it ever was.

BOO: Put that stuff away. He's coming any minute!

REBA: Well, he's not coming on an inspection tour!

BOO: I don't want him to think we live in a pigsty. The Weils are famous for being meticulously neat. Where's Sunny?

REBA: Up in her room studying.

BOO: Good. I want these children to have privacy.

REBA: From Sunny?

BOO: From everybody.

REBA: All right. I sure hope you don't have a stroke before he gets here.

BOO: How thoughtful of you.

(Reba puts the umbrella in the hall closet. Adolph comes down the steps. He wears a hand-knit argyll sweater-vest.)

REBA *(Touched)*: Adolph! You didn't have to wear that!

ADOLPH: I want to. I love it. Thank you.

REBA: Were you surprised?

ADOLPH: Floored.

REBA: I only worked on it while you were at the office or in my room late at night. I was frightened to death Boo would spill the beans.

(A scornful noise from Boo in the living room.)

ADOLPH: Well, she managed to contain herself.

REBA: Now I want you to promise me that you'll only wear it when you feel like it.

ADOLPH: I promise.

REBA: Because I can give it to the thrift shop. I wouldn't mind.

ADOLPH: Reba, please! I'm crazy about it.

(Adolph goes into the dining room and picks at the coffee cake with his fingers. Boo notices.)

BOO: What are you doing? Stop that! *(She hurries in and snatches the cake plate away)* Oh God! Oh Goddy!

ADOLPH: It's only a cake.

BOO: It's a kuchen! It's Grandma's kuchen! And you ruined it!

(The front doorbell sounds. Boo sticks the cake back on the table.)

BOO *(Calling in her musical voice)*: Lala! Company! *(Then to Adolph in her regular one)* Go on.

(Adolph opens the door. Peachy Weil enters. He is in his middle twenties—self-important with bright red hair.)

PEACHY *(Sticking out his hand)*: Peachy Weil.

ADOLPH *(Taking it)*: Adolph Freitag. Come on in.

PEACHY: My cousin Harmon says you're a worse golfer than he is.

ADOLPH: That's sayin' a lot. Harmon's pretty bad. You play?

PEACHY: Varsity at Tulane three years running.

ADOLPH: Sorry I asked.

(Peachy follows Adolph to the living room.)

PEACHY: Nice Chanukah bush.

REBA: Lala decorated almost the whole thing by herself.

PEACHY: You the mother?

REBA: The aunt. By marriage.

BOO: Hidey, Sylvan. I'm Beulah Levy.

PEACHY: Good to see ya.

BOO: My! You certainly do take after the Zacharias side of your family! I'd recognize that hair anywhere.

REBA: It's an attention grabber, all right!

PEACHY: Keeps me outta trouble, my mother says.

ADOLPH: And is she right?

PEACHY: Lemme put it this way—what she don't know won't hurt her.

BOO: Now, congratulations are in order, aren't they? Your Aunt Josephine and your Uncle Ike! Imagine—married fifty years!

PEACHY: To one of those two? No thank you!

(Lala comes down the stairs.)

LALA: Well, goodness me! They seem to be lettin' all kindsa trash into decent people's homes these days.

PEACHY: Hey, Lala.

LALA: Hey? That's what they feed the horses—and the asses.

BOO: Lala!

PEACHY: She always this sassy?

LALA: Me? You oughta hear some of the things Peachy comes out with! He's downright terrible!

BOO: Won't you have some coffee cake, Sylvan?

PEACHY: Does it have nuts in it?

BOO: Pecans. Why?

PEACHY: I'm allergic to nuts. I would die if I ate a pecan.

BOO: Oh, no!

ADOLPH: Well, I wouldn't. *(He goes into the dining room and hacks himself a hefty piece of the kuchen, which he proceeds to eat standing up at the table)*

BOO: Well, you're gonna hafta excuse us. We have a mountain of work to do. Our maid up and quit on us. At this

time of year, too. Did you ever hear of such a thing?
(She pokes Reba)
REBA: Oh, yes! Excuse us!
BOO: I'm so sorry about the pecans! I had no idea!
PEACHY: Don't give it a second thought.

(Boo and Reba go into the dining room, pulling closed the sliding doors. Lala and Peachy are alone.)

LALA: Would you really? I mean, die?
PEACHY: What do you think?

(Peachy looks at Lala, straight-faced, and then he smirks. She laughs.)

LALA: Why did you say that?
PEACHY: Just came out of my mouth. I know. I'm terrible.
LALA: You really are.
PEACHY: My sophomore-year roommate really did.
LALA: Did what?
PEACHY: Have a nut allergy. And somebody put peanut butter in a chocolate cake and didn't tell him.
LALA: What happened?
PEACHY: He died right at the dinner table.
LALA: Oh no! Really?
PEACHY: What do you think?
LALA: Go home! Go home right this minute!
PEACHY: I can't.
LALA: Why?
PEACHY: I have to tell you something. That's why I came over.
LALA: Tell me what?
PEACHY: I can't take you to Ballyhoo tomorrow night.
LALA: What?
PEACHY: I can't take you to Ballyhoo.

LALA: Why?

PEACHY: I have to take somebody else.

LALA: Who?

PEACHY: My cousin Sally Myers—from Columbus.

LALA: Oh. *(A last hope)* Are you making this up, Peachy?

PEACHY: I wish I was. I feel terrible. But there's nothing I can do. They're forcing me.

LALA: Forcing you?

PEACHY: Dad, Uncle Ike, all of them. Sally doesn't know anybody in Atlanta and she's dying to go.

LALA: Can't somebody else take her?

PEACHY: There aren't any other single men in the family. Mother said she was sure you'd understand.

LALA: Did she?

PEACHY: I guess it won't be so bad. Sally's a nifty little dancer.

LALA: Good.

PEACHY: You do understand, don't you?

LALA: I guess.

PEACHY: Good girl. You all right?

LALA: Of course. I'm fine.

PEACHY: Listen, I hate to do this, but I have to ask you something, okay? I don't know anybody else to ask.

LALA: All right.

PEACHY: Should I buy her a white orchid or a purple orchid?

LALA: What color is her dress?

PEACHY: How the hell would I know?

LALA: Then I guess white.

PEACHY: White. Thanks.

LALA: Unless she's wearing black. Then purple.

PEACHY: Oh, I'm pretty sure she won't be wearing black.

LALA: Why?

PEACHY: She's nine years old.

LALA: What?

PEACHY: I swear. My cousin Sally is nine years old.

LALA: Your family is making you take a nine-year-old to Ballyhoo?

PEACHY: What do you think?

LALA: I—I—

PEACHY: Ha ha!

LALA: You're terrible!

PEACHY: Be ready at nine tomorrow night.

LALA: Nine?

PEACHY: Because I'll be here at ten. *(He starts to leave)* What color are you wearing?

LALA: Not black.

PEACHY: Then I'll be sure to get purple.

LALA: You're terrible!

PEACHY: You said it! Bye, sassy ass.

(He goes out the front door.
Boo enters from the kitchen with a piece of choco-
late cake.)

BOO *(In her musical voice)*: Sylvan, I was wondering if I could offer you a piece of—well, where is he?

LALA: He's gone.

BOO: Oh no! What happened?

LALA: Nothing. It's all right. He's taking me to Ballyhoo.

BOO: Well now, you see? And I don't know what you were talking about. He's a lovely boy!

(Lights out.)

SCENE FOUR

The next night.
Peachy and Joe sit side by side on the sofa. Peachy is
wearing a tuxedo and holding an orchid corsage in a see-
through box. Joe has on a dark suit, no flowers. Adolph is
sitting in his customary chair reading the evening paper.
Joe breaks the silence.

JOE: Howza' war news, Mr. A.?

ADOLPH: Not good.

JOE: Yeah. I got relatives over there.

ADOLPH: Poland?

JOE: Unh-hunh. And Russia.

ADOLPH: Well, let's hope for the best.

JOE: Yep.

PEACHY: Let's hope they can dodge bullets.

JOE: Excuse me?

PEACHY: Hey! Easy there, bud! None of this mess is my
fault. It ain't even my problem.

JOE: That right?

PEACHY: You bet. It's Europe's problem and they gotta solve it on their own. Right, Adolph?

ADOLPH: I'd say that depends on where your family is.

PEACHY: Well, mine's been in Louisiana for a hundred and fifty years.

(Reba hurries down the stairs.)

REBA: She's ready.

PEACHY: Which one?

JOE: Mine.

(Joe goes into the hall as Sunny comes down the stairs. She is dressed simply but well. She looks great.)

JOE *(Pleased)*: Hi there.

SUNNY: Hi.

JOE: Terrific.

SUNNY: Thank you.

JOE: Sorry about the monkey suit. Nobody told me.

SUNNY: You'll do.

JOE: Messed up on the flowers, too.

SUNNY: I'll manage to survive.

BOO *(Coming down the stairs)*: Here we come, ready or not!

JOE *(To Peachy)*: Prepare yourself, bud.

(Peachy, corsage box in hand, comes out into the hall. Lala sails down the stairs and poses at the bottom.)

PEACHY: Say! I thought this shindig was formal! Why didn't you get dressed up?

BOO: Why, Sylvan! You are a devil!

LALA: I told you, Mama.

PEACHY: I picked you a posey. *(He presents Lala with the corsage)*

LALA: Oh! Oh! Look! Two! Two white orchids! *(She holds up the large corsage)*
BOO: Adolph, come see!

(Adolph reluctantly rises and joins the group.)

REBA *(Looking at the young people)*: I wish I had a camera!
ADOLPH: You do have a camera, Reba.
REBA: I do?
ADOLPH: You have Simon's Leica. The one he bought in Germany.
REBA: That? I gave it to the thrift shop last summer.
ADOLPH: That was a very expensive camera.
REBA: I know, but nobody ever used it. What did we need it for? Y'all gonna have to excuse me. I still haven't fin- . ished Sunny's sweater! I better get busy. Have fun. I won't wait up.
SUNNY *(To Joe)*: That means she will. 'Night, Mama.

(She goes up the stairs)

ADOLPH: Have fun, y'all.
LALA *(To Sunny and Joe)*: See you there.

(Sunny and Joe exit. Boo pins the corsage and helps Lala into her wrap.)

PEACHY: I forgot. Dorothy says hey.
LALA: Dorothy who?
PEACHY: Dorothy Stein. My cousin Tony's wife.
BOO: From Louisville?

(Peachy nods.)

Lovely people.

LALA: I can't place her. What was her name before?

PEACHY: Beats me. Says she was in your dorm at Michigan.

LALA *(Alarmed)*: Dorothy Wolf? Dotty Wolf from Shaker Heights?

PEACHY: That's the one. Were you in the same sorority with her or something? I know she said it was one or the other—

(Lala faints.)

PEACHY: My God! What did I say?

BOO *(Very calm)*: Nothing. Nothing at all. She didn't eat any dinner is all this is. Plus a little overexcitement. Girls do this all the time. She'll be fine.

PEACHY: She will?

(Lala stirs a bit.)

BOO: I tell you what, Sylvan. Why don't you go on out and warm up the car for Lala? This is a very light evening wrap. I'm 'fraid she'll freeze before y'all get to the club!

PEACHY: Okay, but are you sure she—

BOO: She's fine. She'll be right out. Go on. Go on now.

(Peachy exits.)

LALA: I'm not going.

BOO: Of course you are!

LALA: You don't understand, Mama! Dotty Wolf rushed Sigma Delta Tau with me. And she got in!

BOO: Oh Lord! That was years ago. Maybe she's forgotten about it.

LALA: No she hasn't.

BOO: How do you know that?

LALA: I know Dotty.

BOO: Well, maybe she'll keep quiet out of the kindness of her heart.

LALA: Dotty Wolf? Never in this world. I'm not going! I'm not!

BOO: You've made some very bad decisions about your life. Don't let this be another one.

LALA: Mama! I won't go to Ballyhoo and have people laugh at me!

BOO: If they're gonna laugh at you, they'll do it whether you go or not. At least show a little backbone, for God's sake! We're not weak people! Now you get yourself up and go on out to that car!

LALA: I can't!

BOO: You have to!

LALA: No!

BOO: Well, I guess you're right. Dotty Wolf probably does remember and she probably will tell. And everybody you know will be sayin', "Lala Levy didn't get into Sigma Delta Tau at Michigan. What an awful pill she is!"

LALA: Mama!

BOO: And then they'll say, "Not only that. She had a fit and fell down on the floor in front of that Weil boy and she acted so crazy she couldn't go to the last night of Ballyhoo."

LALA: You are just hateful!

BOO: But I'm right. And pretty soon it'll be "Lala Levy? I don't believe she's been out of that house on Habersham Road for—why it must be twenty years now." Do you see any other possibilities, daughter?

(No answer.)

Well, go on upstairs and work on that radio script. I'm sorry. It's a novel this week, isn't it? Just leave the dress on my bed, sugar. I'll take it back to Rich's tomorrow.

*(Lala hesitates a moment, then grabs her evening wrap
and exits through the front door.
   Adolph reenters.)*

BOO: I don't know—maybe I should've just let her stay at
   home.

ADOLPH: Maybe.

BOO: But I don't know how many more chances she's gonna
   have. She was lucky to get this one.

ADOLPH: Yes.

BOO: You ever stop and think how funny it is, Adolph?

ADOLPH: What?

BOO: That the two of us ended up living together.

ADOLPH: Yeah.

BOO: I never dreamed of anything like this when we were
   little.

ADOLPH: Me either.

BOO: I thought we were gonna be happy when we grew up.

ADOLPH: Unh-hunh.

BOO: What do you think happened?

ADOLPH: I don't know, Boo. I honestly don't know.

(Lights fade on them.)

SCENE FIVE

In the darkness we hear Jerome Kern's "All the Things You Are" played by a dance orchestra.
Sunny and Lala enter, followed by Joe and Peachy.

LALA *(Pulling at Sunny)*: Come on. I'm fixin' to wet right through every single one of my petticoats!

SUNNY: Okay. *(To Joe)* Don't go anywhere.

JOE: Not a chance.

LALA *(To Peachy)*: And you! Behave yourself.

PEACHY: Why, whatever can you mean?

LALA *(Calling offstage)*: Patsy! Wait! You won't believe what just happened! *(She drags Sunny offstage with her)*

PEACHY: You know, I never can figure it out.

JOE: What's that?

PEACHY: Girls always go off to pee in groups. Why do you suppose that is?

JOE: No idea.

PEACHY: You think somethin' funny goes on in the ladies' room that guys don't know about?

JOE: I doubt it.

PEACHY: I mean, what if I grabbed your arm and pulled you off so we could go and take a leak together?

JOE: That's never gonna happen.

PEACHY: Right! My point exactly! *(A beat)* First time at the Standard Club?

JOE: Unh-hunh.

PEACHY: Nice, ain't it?

JOE: It's all right.

PEACHY: Lot better than the Progressive Club, I bet.

JOE: The what?

PEACHY: Progressive Club.

JOE: What's that?

PEACHY: You're shittin' me! How long you been livin' in Atlanta?

JOE: Month or so.

PEACHY: And none of your friends ever took you to the Progressive Club?

JOE: No.

PEACHY: I thought that's where you people went.

JOE: Us people?

PEACHY: The other kind. You know—Russian, Orthodox.

JOE: Wait a sec. Let me get this straight. So the—whaddayacallit—Progressive Club—is where me and the rest of the other kind belong.

PEACHY: Thass right.

JOE: And this one—the Standard Club—?

PEACHY: Us. German Jews.

JOE: German Jews only?

PEACHY: Well, they're startin' to let in a few others because they need the initiation fees. But they try to only take the ones that are toilet trained. At least that's the way my Uncle Ike puts it.

JOE: Sunny knows all this, right?

PEACHY: Knows it? Her uncle's the goddamn past president! So you got nothin' to worry about. You'll be treated like a prince tonight.

JOE: Ah, the hell with it.

(Joe exits. Sunny enters, looking for him.)

SUNNY: Joe?

PEACHY: Probably goin' to take a leak. *(Calls after him)* Don't worry. I ain't comin' with you.

(Lights fade.)

SCENE SIX

The Freitag house. Several hours later. The house is dark, except for a table lamp in the hall.
   Sunny enters through the front door.

SUNNY *(Calling offstage)*: I'm in.

   (Adolph, in his bathrobe, comes into the dining room holding a refrigerator dish full of fried chicken.)

ADOLPH: Sunny?

SUNNY: It's me.

ADOLPH: I thought you were going to a breakfast after the dance.

SUNNY: I asked Harold Lillienthal to bring me home.

ADOLPH: Harold Lillienthal? Where's Joe?

SUNNY: I don't know.

ADOLPH: What happened?

SUNNY: We were dancing and I excused myself and when I came out of the ladies' room, he was gone.

ADOLPH: That doesn't make any sense. Was he feeling all right?

(The doorbell sounds. Adolph opens the door. Joe comes into the front hall. He is missing his usual buoyancy.)

ADOLPH: Joe! You all right?

JOE: Yeah. Sure.

SUNNY: What happened to you?

JOE: I went for a drive.

SUNNY: A drive?

JOE: Yeah.

SUNNY: Why?

JOE: Seemed like the best thing to do.

SUNNY: I see. Well, good night. *(She starts up the stairs)*

JOE: Yeah. Good night. *(He starts for the door)*

ADOLPH: Anybody want a piece of chicken? Good cold.

JOE: No thanks, Mr. A.

ADOLPH: Shame to let it go to waste. Sunny?

SUNNY: I'm not hungry.

ADOLPH: Seems to me a little snack always enhances a late-night discussion.

SUNNY: We're not having a discussion.

ADOLPH: So I notice, but you should be. *(He starts up the stairs)* Holler, now, if you change your mind about the chicken.

(Adolph exits up the stairs. A little silence. Joe clears his throat.)

SUNNY: What?

JOE: I didn't say anything.

SUNNY: Well, you certainly should!

JOE: Should what?

SUNNY: Tell me what happened!

JOE: I bet you've got a pretty good idea.

SUNNY: I don't! I don't at all! I thought we were having a good time!

JOE: We were. And you're wrong.

SUNNY: Wrong?

JOE: You are a good dancer.

SUNNY: Thank you.

JOE: You're welcome.

SUNNY: Joe, I'm entitled to know what happened.

JOE: Why didn't you tell me?

SUNNY: Tell you what?

JOE: Guys like me aren't welcome at the Standard Club.

SUNNY: Is that what all this fuss is about? For heaven's sake! I don't run the Standard Club!

JOE: You took me there.

SUNNY: I wanted to dance with you. I didn't think it mattered.

JOE: Oh really? You planning on taking a swim in that Venetian Club pool any time soon?

SUNNY: It's not at all the same thing.

JOE: Sure it is. You think I like being where I'm not wanted?

SUNNY: You are wanted! Just about anybody can join the Standard Club these days.

JOE: Great! Is that supposed to make me feel better?

SUNNY: You're making an awful lot over nothing, you know.

JOE: Nothing?

SUNNY: Yes. If you'd said something, we could've discussed it. And I could've explained.

JOE: Yeah? Explained what?

SUNNY: That old other kind business—sure, I grew up in a house full of it, but that doesn't automatically mean I believe it myself. As far as I'm concerned, you and I are on equal footing—in every way possible!

JOE: Spoken like a true Wellesley girl! A believer in Upton Sinclair and a fighter for the underdog! You make me sick.

SUNNY: You make me sick! All this about the way you felt. What about the way I felt? I had everybody in the place looking for you. I've never been so embarrassed in my life.

JOE: Tough.

SUNNY: Men don't abandon girls like that where I come from.

JOE *(Sarcastic southern accent)*: Mah deepest apologies, ma'am!

SUNNY: You think this is funny? Of course you do. How could you know any better?

JOE: Wait a minute. How could I know any better?

SUNNY: No! Wait! I—

JOE: Thank you very much. Yeah. Okay. I get it.

SUNNY: We were brought up differently. That's all I mean.

JOE: I know what you mean. You smell like a rose and I smell like a salami sandwich.

SUNNY: I didn't say that. You're not listening to what I'm trying to—

JOE: I'm listening real good and you know what I hear? Jew-hater talk—clear as a bell! Oh yeah, I been hearing that garbage all my life, but damned if I thought I'd ever hear it coming out of a Jewish girl.

SUNNY: How dare you! Storming into this house in the middle of the night and swearing and yelling and accusing me of all kinds of absurd—

JOE: Right! Whyn't you just call me a kike and get it over with?

SUNNY: I think it is over with.

(Joe walks to the door.)

JOE: A shaynim donk in pupik.

SUNNY: I don't know what you're saying.

JOE: Thanks for nothing.

(Joe leaves. Sunny goes up the stairs.
The house is quiet. Then the doorbell sounds. It
sounds again insistently. And again.
A light in the upstairs hall. Adolph comes down-
stairs as the bell keeps sounding. He opens the door.
Lala comes into the front hall. She seems even more
agitated than usual.)

LALA *(Calling)*: Mama! Mama!
ADOLPH: Lala, what is it?
LALA *(Calling)*: Mama!

(Boo, pulling on her robe, rushes down the stairs.
Reba, also in a robe, follows right behind her.)

LALA: Oh, Mama!

(She starts to cry. Boo embraces her.)

BOO: Lala! What happened?

(More tears.)

BOO: Was it that Wolf girl from Michigan?
LALA: No. Dotty didn't say a word.
BOO: Then what is it?
LALA: Peachy asked me to marry him!
BOO: Thank the Lord! Oh, sugar! *(She starts to cry. Then stops)* Are you sure?
LALA: What do you mean am I sure? Of course I'm sure!

(Peachy comes into the hall.)

LALA: She doesn't believe me.
BOO: Is it really true, Sylvan?

PEACHY: What do you think?

REBA: This is such a surprise! When did y'all decide?

PEACHY: We've been talking about it since Thanksgiving.

LALA: We have?

PEACHY: Not you. Mother and Daddy and me.

ADOLPH: Ain't love grand?

BOO: Adolph!

PEACHY: And Daddy said, "Well at least we know what we're gettin' here, all the way back on both sides" and Mother said, "You can have her if you want her, I guess." She was ready to get Grandma Zacharias's engagement ring out of the safe-deposit box for me to bring to Atlanta, but I said let's wait awhile just in case somebody better turns up at Ballyhoo.

LALA: Isn't he awful?

ADOLPH: He certainly is.

LALA: Tell him, Peachy.

ADOLPH: What?

LALA: This is the best part.

PEACHY: I might be interested in movin' to Atlanta and comin' to work with you at the Dixie Bedding Corporation.

BOO: Sylvan! I can hardly believe it! Aren't you thrilled, Adolph?

ADOLPH: What do you think?

(Lights out.)

SCENE SEVEN

In the dark, we hear a conductor's voice.

CONDUCTOR: The station is Wilmington. Wilmington, Delaware, coming up. This station is Wilmington.

(Lights up on the sleeping compartment of the Crescent Limited. It is two weeks later. Sunny is on her way back to college. She is reading a book.
A knock on the door.)

SUNNY: Come in.

(Joe enters.)

JOE: Hi.
SUNNY: Hi.
JOE: So. Your mother finished the sweater, hunh.
SUNNY: Yes.
JOE: Good for her. Looks nice.

SUNNY: Thank you.

JOE *(Looking at the book)*: Upton Sinclair?

SUNNY: Yes.

JOE: Thought so. *(A beat)* So you didn't get your school-work finished over the vacation, huh?

SUNNY: Not quite. Oh.

JOE: What?

SUNNY: Happy New Year.

JOE: Right. Same to you.

SUNNY: Thank you. *(A beat)* What brings you to Wilmington?

JOE: Looking at a bedsprings factory in the neighborhood.

SUNNY: And as long as you were here, Uncle Adolph told you to come down and give me a look-see.

JOE: Yep. Need anything?

SUNNY: No thank you.

JOE: Okay, then. So long.

SUNNY: Bye.

(Joe turns to leave, then stops.)

JOE: I lied.

SUNNY: What?

JOE: Mr. A. didn't tell me to come. He doesn't even know I'm here.

SUNNY: Oh.

JOE: The bedsprings factory is in West Virginia.

SUNNY: How did you get to Wilmington?

JOE: Drove.

SUNNY: All that way? You must've gotten up at five o'clock in the morning.

JOE: Three-thirty.

SUNNY: No!

JOE: I didn't want to miss the train.

SUNNY: Oh. *(A beat)* I'm glad you didn't.

JOE: Me too.

SUNNY: Joe?

JOE: Yeah?

SUNNY: What you said—about Jew-hater talk—

JOE: Yeah?

SUNNY: I thought about it a lot, and it's not true. How could it be? It would be like hating myself.

JOE: Unh-hunh.

SUNNY: No! Don't you see? It's only ignorance. I don't know anything. There's just a big hole where the Judaism is supposed to be. But I remembered. I do know some Yiddish. I went to my suitemate's house in Chestnut Hill for dinner once and they said it at the table. Shabit Shallim—something like that.

JOE: It's not Yiddish. It's Hebrew. Shabbat Shalom. It's the blessing you say Friday night.

SUNNY: Shabbat Shalom.

(Joe smiles.)

Joe, I should never have taken you to Ballyhoo.

JOE: I asked you, remember?

SUNNY: Yes, but I should have known better. I'm sorry.

JOE: Me too. I didn't need to act like such a jerk.

SUNNY: I don't blame you one bit.

JOE: I miss you like hell!

SUNNY: I miss you too.

JOE: It hurts all the time.

SUNNY: I know.

JOE: So I was hopin' maybe—

SUNNY: Me too.

(They kiss. A good big passionate kiss.)

JOE: What's the matter?

SUNNY: What?

JOE: You're crying.

SUNNY: So are you.

JOE: Must be the diesel smoke.

SUNNY: Uncle Adolph told me I should hold on to you.

JOE: Smart man.

CONDUCTOR: *(Offstage)* All aboard! All aboard!

SUNNY: Oh no!

JOE: Don't worry. This is only the beginning.

SUNNY: Of what?

JOE: Who knows, Sunshine? We got the whole future to choose from.

SUNNY: Yes!

JOE: So think of something really good and we'll just make it happen.

SUNNY: Okay.

(Sunny stands center stage and thinks hard. The lights fade on her.)

SCENE EIGHT

Lights up on the Freitag house. The Christmas tree is gone.
Joe, Adolph, Boo, Reba, Lala and Peachy are seated at the
dinner table.
   Sunny walks into the scene and lights the Sabbath candles.

SUNNY: Baruch atah Adonai Eloheinu melech ha-olam,
   asher kidishanu bemitsvotav, vetsivanu l'hadlik neyr
   shel Shabbat. Shabbat Shalom.
JOE: Shabbat Shalom.
REBA: Shabbat Shalom.
PEACHY: Shabbat Shalom.
LALA: Shabbat Shalom.
BOO: Shabbat Shalom.
ADOLPH: Shabbat Shalom.

   (The candles shine.)

END OF PLAY